COMMUNI-CATION

KEY TO YOUR PARENTS

REX JOHNSON

Harvest House Publishers
Irvine, California 92714

COMMUNICATION—KEY TO YOUR PARENTS

Copyright © 1978 Harvest House Publishers
Irvine, California 92714
Library of Congress Catalog Card Number: 78-61874
ISBN #0-89081-157-1

Printed in the United States of America.

CONTENTS

INTRODUCTION

Have your parents been hassling you lately? Or have you decided that being a parent and hassling kids are the same thing? They've been on your back ever since you were a kid—which you could accept then—but even though you're older they still treat you like they used to when you were in grade school. Only the way they enforce their program has changed.

Or maybe your parents haven't been hassling you and they never have. You've been free to do your own thing for a long time. But you sometimes wish your folks were a little closer, especially when one or more of your friends is friends with their dad or mom.

Maybe you're a member of a smaller group of teens who really enjoy your parents' friendship, enjoy being with them, and can put up with some hassle now and then.

Whether your parents hassle you all the time, some of the time, occasionally, or not at all, if you're interested in getting through the rest of your teen years with less hassle, this book is for you.

I want to show you how what you say and do will affect your parents. You have the ability to act and react in ways that will develop your parents' trust and respect in you or will teach them to mistrust you and retard your growth.

If you enjoy a good relationship with your parents, thank God and continue to enrich that relationship. Now is the best time to build an even better relationship.

To be most helpful, this book should be tried, not just read. If you thumb through the book you'll notice two kinds of response sections in each chapter. **"What do you think?"** sections invite you to think and then write your responses to questions dealing with what you've read. If you stop and respond in writing before you go on, you'll find your reading more helpful and rewarding.

WHAT DO YOU THINK?

What might be some benefits of a better relationship with your folks?

1. _____

_____

2. _____

_____

3. _____

_____

At the end of each chapter, "**What is your plan?**" sections challenge you to try out some of the ideas for size. You'll find that putting ideas to work will make them much easier to remember, and that practicing how you'll act and react to your parents will help keep you cool in crises.

The very best way to use this book is to make it a family project. If your parents will read the companion book to this one (**Communication—Key To Your Teens**), while you read **Communication—Key**

To Your Parents, you'll have plenty of good things to talk about together. In fact, if you plan a weekly "family council" around questions you might ask your parents, you'll find that you will discover even more about yourself and your parents.

I'd like to recommend one other book you or your parents might be interested in. **Building Positive Parent-Teen Relationships** is a teacher's guidebook for a class or seminar on parent-teen relationships. You might suggest it to your pastor or youth minister. It is authored by Norman Wright and me, and published by Harvest House Publishers.

WHAT IS YOUR PLAN?
1. **I could use this book: [check one or more]**
   _____ a) **to help me enrich my relationship with my parents;**
   _____ b) **to build positive relationships with my parents as we work together on Communication—Key To Your Teens and this book;**
   _____ c) **in a class or study group with other teens and my Youth Minister;**
   _____ d) **in a class or study group with other families.**
2. **How are you going to interest your parents in Communication, Key To Your Teens if they're not already interested?**

CHAPTER I

You and Your Parents

Think of all the good things you have going for you: your health, talents, gifts, friends, school, work, heritage, culture and nation are just some that are often taken for granted. How about your family? How high on a specific list of things you have going for you would you put your family?

One of the characteristics of adolescence is changing family relationships. This is natural and not something to be afraid of. In fact, if at eighteen a teenager has exactly the same relationship with his family that he had when he was thirteen, something would be wrong.

But many parents and teenagers fear adolescence because they equate changed relationships with alienation. In their view, adolescence is a time to "become your own person" or to stand on your own two feet." So of course that means good-by to closeness and doing things together and talking it over, right? **No!** Just because relationships change doesn't mean that they have to get worse. For some families, the teen years are the closest and best. What makes some families strong? What causes other families to fracture? Most important, how can your family become one of the most important things you have going for you? Let's take these questions one at a time, starting with things that make a family strong.

FAMILY STRENGTHENERS

If you were to talk to fifty strong families about what made their family strong you would probably come up with two hundred ways to build strong families. Which would be right for your family? And where would you start? After all, how much change can you make in your family? Isn't that your parents' responsibility?

A more practical way to begin might be to look into Scripture to discover some principles that are applicable to family life, and then apply them yourself. You can cause profound changes in your family even though you're not the family leader. As a family member **you** can initiate these changes and be a leader in your home.

Galatians 5:22-23 reads, **But the fruit of the Spirit is love, joy, peace, patience, kindness, goodness, faithfulness, gentleness, self-control; against such things there is no law.**

This passage is written to every Christian, not just heads of families. You will find that if you listen to the Holy Spirit as He prompts you, you will discover ways to live the fruit of the Spirit in your home. As a result, you will find your family growing stronger. Your home is a great place to make Scripture come alive. For one reason, your family knows you intimately, so it's difficult to put them on. Second, they will be more honest with you about yourself than your friends will. Third, they will be more likely to notice changes in the way you live, especially little changes that make a lot of difference.

Since these qualities are the fruit of the Holy Spirit, and the Holy Spirit lives in everyone who claims Jesus as Lord, then these qualities are true descriptions of every real Christian. Look over the list again. Do these qualities always describe you—especially in your home? Do you know any Christians who are not loving or joyful or gentle or self-controlled?

If Christians can be indwelt by the Holy Spirit and not produce the fruit of the Spirit, then additional growth is an obvious need. But how can a person grow in love, joy, peace and the rest of the qualities listed in Galatians 5:22-23? Let's take them one at a time and consider some ways.

LOVE - In John 13:35 Jesus designates love as the label by which men can tell we are His disciples. The most obvious description of a strong family is that each family member loves the others. But maybe love is such an obvious requirement for family strength that it is assumed.

After describing love so beautifully in 1 Corinthians 13, the first thing Paul says in 1 Corinthians 14 is "pursue love." Then in Colossians 3:14 Paul says, **"And beyond all these things put on love, which is the perfect bond of unity."**

Love is active. Is your love active? How do your dad and mom know you love them? Doing your chores and not hassling your parents don't qualify as answers to these questions. Active love goes beyond the chores and the ordinary to the creative.

One teenager took his dad to the ball game, even paying the parking fee and buying hot dogs. Another teenager we know is crocheting a blanket for her parents' bed. Other teenagers have brought flowers home to mom, painted a room, watched the younger children so dad and mom could go out for an evening—the list could go on. But you need to make your own list of things you could do to let your folks know you love them. Just remember, what you do should be on your own initiative. You think it up, or borrow one of the ideas you just read. But spring it on them. Don't expect a great response, especially if you've never done anything like this before.

WHAT DO YOU THINK?

1. **Which of the ideas mentioned above would be right for your dad or mom?**

2. **What other ways can you let your folks know you love them? Make a list while they're fresh on your mind.**

JOY is usually thought of as a result, not a quality that can grow in a Christian's life. Sometimes it is! But the command in Philippians 4:4 is to **"Rejoice in the Lord always; again I will say, rejoice!"** Another way to say "rejoice" is to say "be joyful again"—it's a command!

It is interesting to notice that the Bible expects us to be joyful again especially when it is difficult to rejoice. In Philippians 2:18 Paul urges Christians to rejoice in the same way he does. James 1:2 says, **"Consider it all joy, my brethren, when you encounter various trials."**

How do we strengthen our family with joy? One way is to be joyful when the going is tough. For instance, those times Dad has to say "no" to a request are much easier to handle if you rejoice even though disappointed. Try rejoicing when your dad or mom gives you extra work to do, it's much easier on your emotions than grouching! Try rejoicing when your folks won't let you stay out as late as you wanted to. It's not the natural thing to do—it's supernatural; but so are you!

PEACE is another family strengthener if you build it rather than just expecting it. Peace is much more than the absence of hassle. As the peace of Christ strengthens you it will have the effect of peacefulness in your family, too. But beyond that, you can let the peace of Christ rule in your family, even if other family members don't. For instance, rather than continuing to try to get the last word in an argument, try letting Christ's peace rule in your own heart, and allow the other person to have the last word. Take your appeal to your referee—the peace of Christ.

When someone in your family has been unfair, hasn't played by the rules, when you've been fouled—those are times to appeal to your referee—the peace of Christ!

What is the peace of Christ? In John 16:33 Jesus explains that He has told His disciples all that is recorded in John 15 and 16 so that they could have peace **in Him.** Then He said, **"In the world you have tribulation, but take courage; I have overcome the world."** The peace of Christ is that we are **in Him** and that He has overcome the world.

PATIENCE - What a family strengthener patience is! And God wants us to develop patience so much that He tells us in Romans 5 to exult (leap for joy) when we're hit by tribulation (pressure or stress). We can welcome pressure because God assures us that pressure builds patience.

Patience is an important fruit of the Holy Spirit in our lives because, as Romans 5 goes on to say, patience builds character. We have also done ourselves a favor when we've learned to respond patiently to pressure because patience dramatically reduces pressure. It is like a safety valve on a pressure cooker.

Did you ever notice how when pressure mounts there appears to be less and less choice? Eventually we get to the place where we can only see one way out. The options are all gone. We do what we have to do. Then, so often, we regret what we did. Impatience is ignoring the options that are still there. If this is a common feeling, you still have the need to develop patience.

Your home is a great place to practice patience, because your patience will take the pressure off of people you love as well as off yourself. The best way to develop patience is to keep communicating with the Holy Spirit as the pressure mounts. Ask Him to show you and remind you of the choices you have open to you. Ask Him to guide your thinking and then wait for His answers!

WHAT DO YOU THINK?

You're out shopping with your dad, you still have to wash the car and get dressed, your date is at 7:00, it takes 15 minutes to get to your girlfriend's home, it's 6:00 now and your dad is still talking to the friend he met in the sports department, right? What are your options? 1) **Leave dad at the store—he can walk home; 2) Cut into his conversation and remind him you're in a hurry; 3) Pace up and down the aisle hoping he notices; 4) Wet your pants; 5) Phone your date to tell her you'll be a little late; 6) None of the above; 7) All of the above.**

Can you think of several alternative choices to the ones mentioned above?

_____

KINDNESS - Does kindness run in your family? Do you initiate kindness, or do you leave being kind to your dad or mom? God is so kind that His kindness is called "lovingkindness" in Psalm 51:1, 52:1, 8.

WHAT DO YOU THINK?

1. **Kindness is: (circle your choice)**
   a. **The opposite of being mean;**
   b. **Not punching out your little brother's lights for ruining your date;**
   c. **Quietly letting your dad change the TV channel even though it was your favorite show;**
   d. **Letting someone else be strong.**
   e. **All of the above.**
2. **Some ways you could be kind to your parents are:**
   a. _____

   b. _____

   c. _____

GOODNESS - One of Satan's favorite strategies for confusing people is to make what's good seem bad, and what's bad seem good. First he makes it look as if goodness is no fun. Then being good becomes downright boring! Meantime Satan makes being bad mysterious and adventuresome. Finally we come to the conclusion that being bad is downright advantageous! In the process we lose our perspective and quit following the Holy Spirit so closely.

Isn't it interesting how we appreciate good and reject bad apples, insects, nails, and even football teams, but we change our reasoning when it comes to our behavior. Since Satan has twisted good into bad and vice versa, real goodness is unnatural, or should we say supernatural—a fruit of the Holy Spirit in our lives.

Are we then committed to a life of drudgery? No way! Drudgery is just what awaits us if we buy Satan's life because the consequences of sin is slavery—slavery to the very sin we thought was so mysterious and adventuresome.

But can't we have excitement and freedom at the same time? One way! Jesus has saved us from sin and its slavery. But He has also saved us for goodness and freedom.

Is yours a ''good'' family? What is your contribution to make it better?

FAITHFULNESS

WHAT DO YOU THINK?
1. Faithfulness is (circle your choice)
   a. keeping your promises;
   b. being full of faith;
   c. being trustworthy;

d. **believing in someone;**
e. **all of the above.**

Sometimes it's easier to have faith in someone you don't know than in someone you know well. Some years ago I was a contestant on the TV game show, "Password." My first partner was Elizabeth Montgomery, star of "Bewitched." I had seen her show many times and figured that if she would just twitch her nose we would win. She twitched, we lost! I got to talk to her after the taping of the show and came away liking her as a person rather than a TV star.

We know our family members well enough to know their limitations, their fears, and previous failures. So we often take them for granted, or worse, we expect failure. Of course we are not surprised when we get what we expected. But what might have happened if we had been faithful?

Faithfulness, then, has two sides: 1) our belief in God and in the people He has placed around us, and 2) our trustworthiness and promises kept. The second side makes it easier for those around us to have faith in us.

GENTLENESS - When you think of gentleness, what picture comes to mind? A young mother holding her baby? A gradual ski slope with three inches of new powder? One of my favorite pictures of gentleness is of El Cid, the Spanish hero, having beaten his enemy in a sword duel, refusing to kill an enemy he had reason to hate. His reason for grace was "anyone can take life; it takes a man to give life." El Cid was a gentleman.

When you could win an argument with a strong and forceful comment but you hold your tongue, that's gentleness. When you open the door and carry the grocery bags into the house for your mom, that's gentleness. When you carry the trash cans out to the curb for your Dad, that's gentleness.

Gentleness is sometimes confused with weakness, but there's actually a lot of difference. Giving in to the impulse to make the argument-winning comment is weakness. It takes strength to be gentle, and that is the fruit of the Holy Spirit.

SELF-CONTROL - The last fruit of the Spirit is another tremendous strengthener. A family in which each member is self-controlled doesn't have to strive to control each other, or to break free from each other.

The alternatives to self-control are impulsiveness and control by others. Young children are by nature impulsive. So to keep them from self-inflicted harm, their parents must control their behavior. Obviously, that creates conflict. As children learn self-control, parents can relax their controls. There are a lot of factors that muddy up the picture, but one thing is for sure — the teenager who is learning self-control will be a much better man or woman and will usually have a much happier time as a teenager than the one who ignores self-control!

FAMILY FRACTURERS

Just as you can cause profound changes that will strengthen your family, you can also be the person that fractures a family.

We've been looking at family strengtheners in Galatians 5:22-23. The family fracturers are listed in Galatians 5:19-21.

"Now the deeds of the flesh are evident, which are: immorality, impurity, sensuality, idolatry, sorcery, enmities, strife, jealousy, outbursts of anger, disputes, dissensions, factions, envyings, drunkenness, carousings and things like these . . ."

Now who would admit to a list like this? You probably wouldn't describe any of your friends, much less yourself with this list. But how important is it to you to express all your feelings? How important is it that you get your own way? How important is having a good time?

Nobody's saying that having a good time, expressing your feelings, or even getting your own way is sinful! But we have a way of redefining sin so it doesn't sound so bad when we do it, don't we? What's wrong with a little fun—like a wild party now and then, especially around Christmas and New Year's Eve? So we got a little drunk. Nobody got hurt, so what's so sinful? Galatians 5:21 calls this kind of activity drunkenness and carousing.

What we call expressing our feelings might sometimes more appropriately be called impurity, sensuality or even immorality, and at other times jealousy and outbursts of anger. Then we redefine words like enmities, strife, disputes, dissensions, and factions as what we have to do to achieve our objectives and get what we want.

Should we then deny our feelings, never have a good time, never set or achieve any objectives, never have our own way? It would be a shame to miss out on God's best by jumping to such conclusions. Notice that each of the "deeds of the flesh" listed in Galatians 5:19-21 are things people do for themselves at the expense of other people. They are ways of saying, "I love myself and I want you to help me love myself."

This is how these deeds fracture families. One or more family members demand that the rest help him love himself, and the problems begin. Pretty soon family members are competing for each other's love. As love gets more and more scarce, the competition gets more and more fierce. Eventually one or more family members goes outside the home to find love.

HOW TO MAKE YOUR FAMILY YOUR GREATEST ASSET?

WHAT DO YOU THINK?

1. If you didn't already put your family at the top of the list of things you've got going for you, what would it take for them to achieve that importance? What would have to happen to make your family your most important asset?

a. _____

_____

b. _____

_____

c. _____

Chances are your answers to the questions above were changes that other members in your family need to make, over which you have no control. Right? If they are changes you can make, especially ones you can make all by yourself, great! If not, how can your family become your greatest asset?

Your family is like a gold mine. Buried beneath the

surface are riches that will last a lifetime. But they must be mined! That means you must invest time, energy and creativity in your family. It won't yield its benefits to you until you've taken the initiative and invested. The more you invest, the greater the reward! Maybe it will take a long time, a lot of energy and creativity before you strike ore, but keep digging—it's worth it.

But your family's all played out, you say? All the more reasons to invest more time, energy, and creativity! The way it works is like this: family members get used to each other and adapt slowly to each other's gradual changes. But any rapid change one member makes puts the system out of balance. It's as if they have to live with a new and different person. If this person is easier to live with than the one they are used to, they change, too. A teenager who is following the guidance of the Holy Spirit is certainly easier to live with than one who is on his own road.

So if you've been waiting for someone in your family to change, your wait is over. You change—start investing, and your family will have to adapt to the new you. You'll be one of the winners, especially in the long run.

How should you change? The rest of this book will suggest all sorts of ways you can change that will make it easy for the rest of your family to change too. Of course, you may be entirely satisfied with your life the way it is, and not want to change. You may even be afraid of change. If so, you're the one that will miss out!

WHAT IS YOUR PLAN?

1. Which of the qualities listed in the fruit of the Spirit in Galatians 5:22-23 do you think you have the most of?

2. How could you express that quality to each of your family members in a way they would appreciate it?

   a. Dad _____

   _____

   b. Mom _____

   _____

   c. Brothers or sisters _____

   _____

3. In which quality do you need the most growth?

4. Plug your answer to number 3 into the following growth plan.

   a. Find as many Scripture references as you can that say something about the quality you're working on. Ask your church librarian to loan you a concordance if you need help.

   b. Ask God to place you into situations with your family where you can use your quality.

   c. Keep track of each time that fruit of the Holy Spirit is obvious to you and you'll be charting your growth.

CHAPTER II

I Gotta Be Me

Who are you? When someone asks you who you are, you usually start with your name, right? Then you might add information about some of your activities such as school or work and some of your associations such as club, choirs or teams.

Little children can be anybody they want to be—Superman, Batman, O.J. Simpson, Farrah Fawcett-Majors; the names change yearly. Sometimes they are "Daddy" or "Mommy" and give their own names to dolls or stuffed animals. Who were the heroes you pretended to be when you were five years old? Remember them?

WHAT DO YOU THINK?

1. Who are some of the people you admire?

2. What do these people have that you would like to have?

3. If you could change one thing about yourself, what would it be?

4. **Try writing some one-word descriptions of your-self.**

   a. _____

   b. _____

   c. _____

   d. _____

   e. _____

5. **Now look back over your descriptions, and put a + next to each word that is complimentary, and a — next to each word that is negative.**
6. **Are any of these words the way you hope to be rather than the way you really are?**

Names are like the labels that come on new clothes. They give us a way of identifying ourselves and other people around us. My "last name" is Johnson. The label "Johnson" identifies my family. The label "Rex" distinguishes me from the other members of the Johnson family. Since there are many other Johnsons running around, and even some other Rex Johnsons, I've been given some other labels, too. Officially, I'm identified by my social security number, driver's license number and some credit card numbers.

Some of my labels are husband, daddy, professor, speaker, author, skier, student, tall, dark, moustached, winner, minister. Notice how positive these labels are. When I see myself wearing one or more of these labels I feel confident and successful.

Then there are other labels I wear sometimes. Some of these are overweight, almost bald, busy, inadequate, loser, defensive, slow. Notice how negative these labels are. When I see myself wearing one or more of these labels I feel inadequate, afraid, and unsuccessful.

Where do these labels come from? Why do I accept some labels and not others? Are labels given me or can I choose them? Can I change labels or am I stuck with the ones I already have? Appropriate answers to these questions can mean the difference between enjoying life or fearing it, between healthy family relationships or poor ones, and between personal growth or regression.

CHOOSING LABELS

As we grow up we not only hear our names we hear parents and other people give us labels. For instance, we hear "Mary is a good student." "Johnny's always late." "Jim is a bad boy." "Jane is always so quiet." As some of these labels are repeated, we begin to believe them. Then we start living up to them and finding ways of getting people to confirm what we believe. Finally we "buy" the label.

Mary is not **always** a good student. Sometimes she's downright flaky! But if she hears people saying she is a good student often enough, she begins to believe it. Then Mary starts living up to what she believes about herself—she studies hard.

The idea that we buy our labels is important. It means that we invest something in building up an idea of what we are like. If we choose to invest in negative labels like "inadequate," "slow," or "bad" we protect our investment just as much as if we choose positive labels like "adequate," "competent" or "good."

YOU CAN CHANGE LABELS

The first thing to remember is that labels have alternatives, and that you are not **always** best described by the labels you have chosen. If you have chosen "inadequate" as a label, remember you are **not always** "inadequate." If you've chosen "too tall," "ugly," "shy," or "tall, dark and handsome" as labels you are not always these either.

Secondly, you can change your labels. If you own some labels it is because you have invested in being this way. The trick now is not somehow to disinvest. The way to change is to start investing in new labels—positive ones. You can start by asking the following questions.

WHAT DO YOU THINK?

1. **How do you look? Do you like your appearance? Circle the descriptions below that fit you best.**
   a. **At birth the doctor hit me with an ugly stick. I hate mirrors.**
   b. **My looks keep me from having as many friends as "good looking" kids have.**
   c. **My appearance is sometimes good news, sometimes bad news.**
   d. **I'm happy with my appearance most of the time.**
   e. **I should be a model.**
2. **How do you perform? Do you tend to get As, Bs, Cs, Ds or Fs in life? Give yourself a grade _____.**
3. **Do you wait on people or do people wait on you?**

4. **Do you feel "in" most of the time or left out?**

5. **Which is most correct as far as you are concerned? a) "I'm O.K. - You're O.K.; b) "We're both rotten."**

6. **Do you feel you can handle most of life's sliders and knuckle balls or are you in over your head much of the time? I can handle it___, I can't handle it ___ .**

The possibility of developing a consistently negative self-image and wearing mostly negative labels is enormous. In fact, it is more likely that most teenagers are developing a poor self-image than a good one! This is because when you ask your friends to confirm your perceptions and feelings about yourself they have to cope with both your request and their feelings about themselves. They are biased judges, afraid to tell you the truth unless it happens to be flattering. Even then, to admit that you're good looking, doing well, or "in" is risky because they may feel not so good looking, so able, or so "in."

There is a better way of choosing labels and in time it leads to a very strong, safe identity. You start by going to God for an opinion about yourself rather than to other people. What does God say about you? Beware, though, of going to God for confirmation. If you already have an idea about yourself when you go to God you may hear what you want to hear rather than what He is saying. So you start with what God has already said about you in His Word, the Bible.

About your appearance, God says He knew what

you were going to look like before you were born. Do you wish God would have done a better job on your appearance? Most of us do sometimes! But that's because we focus on the wrong things. We focus on the parts of our body and face that we think people around us focus on. That's because we want their approval of us.

Before you judge God's handiwork, maybe you'd better take another look. It really was God who made you, and God has never made a mistake. You are not a mistake either.

David's response to the realization that God was concerned with his appearance is found in Psalm 139:14. ''I will give thanks to thee, for I am fearfully and wonderfully made; **Wonderful are thy works**, and my soul knows it very well.'' Can you, with David, **thank God** for your appearance? You are God's wonderful work! If you don't agree, it's because you've already made up your mind about your appearance and are going to God for confirmation on your opinion instead of starting with His opinion. Guess who needs to change opinions!

One caution needs to be added about your appearance. God gives you the responsibility to keep it in good shape. So maybe you need to ask the question, ''Did God make me this way or did I make me this way?'' The answer is obvious when you are talking about height, skin color, facial and body features and many other attributes over which you have no control. The answer is questionable when you are talking about weight, complexion, habits, temperaments, dress and grooming.

About your performance, God has a couple of surprises. First, regardless of how hard you try, you will always fall short when it comes to God's standards of excellence. As Fritz Ridenour says in **How To Be A Christian Without Being Religious**, ''God doesn't grade on the curve.''[1] So trying to do well enough to please God is only going to lead to frustration.

The reason God sent Jesus to die on a cross was to make you acceptable and presentable in heaven. When Jesus paid for your sins with His death, He made your shortcomings forgivable. They become forgiven when you accept Jesus' payment for **your** sins. If you've not accepted God's forgiveness yet, maybe it's because you're focusing on the wrong audience. Performing for the people around you may have you so tied down to living up to their expectations that you have forgotten what Jesus already did for you!

If you have accepted God's forgiveness, you may still be trying to live up to His standards. You're probably finding it frustrating. The second surprise God has for you in the area of performance is that you **cannot** live up to His standards any more than can a person who is not one of His children. That is why Philippians 2:13 says ''for it is God who is at work in you, both to will and to work for His good pleasure.'' Jesus did his work on the cross to make all who accept Him acceptable to God. He is also working in you to make you pleasurable to God.

So how are you doing? God says you're doing just fine if you have accepted His forgiveness through Jesus. God says you're doing just fine if you are accepting His present, progressive work in your life.

About your status, God has some very special pronouncements. When you ask God ''How important am I?'', He responds in I Peter 1:18-19, ''knowing that you were not redeemed with perishable things like silver or gold from your futile way of life inherited from your forefathers, but with precious blood . . . the blood of Christ." **You are worth the precious blood of Christ!** That is not just estimated value. That is what God has **already paid** for you.

You are of such high value to God that He gives you the status of being His child when you receive Him. (John 1:12). You are not just another one of a lot of God's children, either. God says in Romans 8:16-17 that you are an heir of God—a fellow heir with Christ. That means that you are also entitled to all the riches that Christ is heir to as God's son. How's that for status?

Knowing what God has done in forming you, forgiving you, and favoring you should make a difference in your feelings about yourself. Does it?

WHAT DO YOU THINK?

1. **Do you feel wanted, accepted, "in" as far as God is concerned? If not, you can belong to His family by asking Jesus to come into your life. He will!**
2. **Do you feel worthy—that you count for something? If not, read Colossians, Chapter I.**
3. **Do you feel competent—that you're able and adequate? In case your adequacy is misplaced, please read Philippians 4:13 and Romans 8:37-39 whether you feel competent or not.**

In a letter to the editor of "Christianity Today" magazine, Rod Martin writes, "The Good News of Christ teaches me to see myself, as well as other people, as God sees us—not only as sinners, but also as essentially valuable persons, created in God's image and redeemed by Christ's precious blood. In Christ I can begin to love and accept myself and others because in Christ God loves and accepts us unconditionally. Only then am I truly freed to forget my selfish preoccupation with false feelings of inadequacy and worthlessness and then I can begin to have God unreservedly and to selflessly minister to the needs of others." [2]

YOUR IDENTITY AND YOUR FAMILY

How you label yourself and how you feel about yourself is important to your family. You not only make life enjoyable or fearful for yourself, your family is influenced by the kinds of labels you invest in and wear.

If you see yourself as inadequate, unable, or struggling to find yourself, then any time a family member compliments you, your suspicion is aroused: "What does he want?" Or when a family member suggests in some way that you need to change you become defensive: "I am not a poor loser." So rather than honest communication existing between family members, suspicion and defensiveness develops. When one family member gets suspicious and defensive, the rest have to cope, and sometimes they become suspicious and defensive, too.

If you invest in and wear positive labels based on your realization of what God thinks of you and the high value He places on you, then you can take compliments in stride and enjoy other family members' company. You can take suggestions that you need to change, weigh them, try these changes, then accept or reject them on the basis of a rational decision. You can even take criticism. When you feel positive about yourself, you can accept criticism, weigh it objectively, determine if it can help you grow, and use it to become a more mature person. In contrast, when you feel poorly about yourself criticism is almost always taken as an attack upon your person, whether it was intended that way or not.

A second way your labels affect your family is if in the past, you have accepted your parents' labels and invested in them, and now find you don't like those labels any more, the tendency is to reject your parents along with the labels.

You don't need to reject your parents or the labels you feel they've stuck you with. Being able to say "I've been inadequate," "I'm sometimes clumsy," is not harmful to your self-image if you can also say "I'm becoming more adequate," and "sometimes I'm poetry in motion!" The trick is to ignore the negative labels and concentrate on the value God places on you as a person.

WHAT IS YOUR PLAN?

1. **What are some negative labels you have worn, and what are some positive alternative labels you might choose to wear instead?**

   a. _____

   _____

   b. _____

   _____

   c. _____

2. We tend to value the things we invest the most in. Do you consider school, involvement in your church, your choice of friends and recreation investments in one of God's children—you? How might you change these investments to get better returns — a more valuable you? List some changes here.

a. _____

_____

b. _____

_____

c. _____

_____

3. What labels have you had for your parents that may be inappropriate and not needed anymore? Can you think of some alternatives?

LABELS   ALTERNATIVES

a. _____   _____

b. _____   _____

c. _____   _____

1. Fritz Ridenour, How To Be A Christian Without Being Religious (Glendale, California: Regal), pp. 9-22.
2. Rod Martin, "Letter To The Editor," Christianity Today Vol. XXII No. 2, (October 21, 1977), pp. 8-9.

CHAPTER III

Are You Communicable?

The scene appears in most war movies and in many westerns—there's a "lull" in the battle and one lone figure appears waving a white cloth. The tension mounts as the moments pass. Will the enemy talk or will the lonely messenger be blown away? You've probably been in the position of wanting to talk but not sure that you want to hear a response. Your dad or mom may be ready for a calm discussion, but on the other hand, you could be blown away! They have been in that position, too—with you!

How would you describe the atmosphere in your home? Would "constant warfare" be a good description? Maybe "cold war" with intermittent firefights would better describe your home. How about no warfare at all, just isolation—two or more worlds on the same property? Would you believe there are teenagers and parents who talk to each other, love each other, and aren't afraid to say so? There are lots of each of these homes; maybe yours is the loving kind.

Probably the most common kind of home is a mixture of the examples just described. It is sometimes loving, sometimes warring, and sometimes isolating. Often, parent-teen relationships are loving with one or two teenagers, but strained with one of their brothers or sisters.

Why is it that some teenagers and parents can get along so well most of the time while others can't? One possible answer is that some parents don't know how to talk with teenagers. Before concluding that this is true for a particular set of parents (yours for instance), a good question would be, "Do they communicate with some teenagers and not with others? If so, maybe they do know how to talk with teenagers.

Another possible answer is that it's the teenagers problem. A family that used to get along so well together has fallen into silence. What's the problem? The child has become a teenager and the interests and concerns have turned outside the home. There's little if anything to talk about.

A third possible answer is that parents and teenagers share the responsibility to communicate and that if there's a lack of communication it's a failure for both.

In reality this third answer is most often accurate. Communication by definition is a two-way process and always involves at least two people. It can break down whenever one person quits talking or listening, but usually a breakdown is two-sided.

WHAT DO YOU THINK?

1. **Is the atmosphere around your home (check one):**
   ____**safe to talk about anything?**
   ____**safe to talk about most things?**
   ____**safe to talk about some things, dangerous with others?**
   ____**dangerous enough to avoid if possible?**
   ____**too dangerous to talk about anything important?**

2. **How would your parents respond to number one? (Write your response, then ask them, if it is safe to do so.)**

MAKE COMMUNICATION POSSIBLE

When a communication breakdown occurs, a most common reaction is to find out who is to blame for the breakdown. Everybody finds someone else to blame. It's always the other guy's fault! Who wants to admit blame and take the heat from everyone concerned? But notice that the focus of blaming is on the past, and usually the most intense blamers are partly to blame themselves. That's why they try to focus everyone's attention on someone else.

Finding out who is to blame for the lack of communication is less helpful than taking responsibility for building communication. A lot of people try to find someone to blame whenever there's a problem so they can give the responsibility for finding a solution to the person who holds the blame. This strategy is absorbed by little children and heard in whines like, "I didn't drop those toys here, my sister did— she should be the one to pick them up." Teenagers continue the strategy with statements like "You forgot to remind me—it's your fault I forgot." "She made me late." "He made me angry."

Forgetting who is to blame and initiating positive action to build communication and loving relationships is a mark of maturity, no matter how old a person is.

If communication is strained or non-existent there are some things you can do to make it easier for your folks to communicate **with** you. Of course there are times when you feel like being alone and quiet—when you **don't** want to talk. But you can communicate that feeling safely, too, if you have set up an atmosphere of safe communication.

What is the atmosphere around you like? Do people near you want to talk to you or do they tend to want to do other things? You know the feeling—it's like when one of your friends has missed a shower or two. The atmosphere around them makes you want to get upwind. Even teenagers who smell good sometimes create an atmosphere that pushes people away. Adults do it too, but let's look at atmospheres that teenagers build and suggest an alternative for each.

PENDULUM CLOCK OR SELF-WINDING WATCH?

Many teenagers make it difficult for parents, other adults and even other teenagers to talk with them because they are like a pendulum clock. Their moods swing back and forth from one extreme to the other so that a parent or friend doesn't know whether it's safe to communicate or not.

Take Bill, for instance, he's working on his car and it's not going together right when his dad gets home. Bill's dad says, "Hi, Bill" and gets nothing more than a cold stare or a grunt. So he walks into the house wondering what's wrong with his son. He avoids talking with Bill the rest of the evening because he doesn't want a hassle and he knows Bill doesn't want one either.

The atmosphere that keeps Bill and his dad from really enjoying each other is one Bill has built by being totally unpredictable. Bill's dad is never sure how Bill will respond so he avoids talking as much as possible.

The alternative to the pendulum clock is the self-winding watch. The teenager who is like the self-winding watch is sometimes all wound up and at other times needs some encouragement. But he is not so unpredictable that he makes his friends and family uncomfortable.

No one is happy, jolly and ''up'' all the time. But the teenager whose mood swings from one extreme to the other frequently pushes people away, whether he means to or not. The Bible shows us how to be a self-winding watch type of Christian. It says, in Philippians 4:4, ''Rejoice in the Lord always, again I will say, rejoice!''

STUBBORN MULE OR INTELLIGENT QUARTER HORSE?

It's fascinating to watch a cowboy and a good quarter horse separating cattle. The horse not only moves immediately upon command, he anticipates the cowboy's commands. Although it might be farfetched to say that the horse figures out what the cowboy will do next, it is safe to say that he picks up cues from the cowboy and the cattle and responds so quickly that it looks like he is able to reason.

Mules, in contrast, seem to have plans of their own. Mules are so independent that they have become symbols in our society of stubbornness. Talking to a mule is a waste of time and energy. All the words in the world won't change a mule's mind once it's made up.

Sometimes the atmosphere for communication that a teenager develops is just plain ''muleish.'' This is true of adults, too, but rather than waiting for dad or mom to change your mind, how about building a better atmosphere for communication? You can do it all by yourself!

Philippians 4:5 says, "Let your forbearing spirit be known to all men. The Lord is near." What is a forbearing spirit? If you had one would you recognize it? The Greek word which is translated "forbearing" has two parts. The second part is the word that is translated "reasonable" in Romans 12:1 (KJV). The first part of the word is a prefix meaning "intensively." Together they mean "intensively reasonable." To paraphrase the first part of the verse we might say, "Build an atmosphere of super-reasonableness." What a contrast to "stubborn mule-ishness!"

An atmosphere of stubborness cuts off communication. An atmosphere of reasonableness keeps communication open. An atmosphere of stubbornness tends to make others around us stubborn too. An atmosphere of reasonableness gives those around us the freedom to change.

CHATTERING BROOK OR QUIET STREAM?

Another atmosphere that makes communication difficult is the noisy one. Just about everybody has been in a place that was so noisy they had to go someplace else to talk. The contrast is that of standing near a chattering brook or roaring waterfall versus standing or sitting next to a quiet stream. Psalm 23:2 says, "He leads me beside quiet waters." Literally, it is "waters of rest."

Sometimes it is exciting to be near a chattering brook or some roaring falls. But communication, especially the kind that is vital to building relationships, is better where there is peace.

Some people are like a chattering brook—always noisy, moving quickly, sort of splashy and comparatively shallow. Usually these people are somewhat anxious. Other descriptions are "high-strung," low ability to concentrate, overly concerned, apprehensive and tense. "Chattering" is also a good description because this person talks a lot. But talking and communicating are not always the same thing. In fact sometimes a lot of talking is a way to avoid sharing our **feelings, needs, or the things which threaten us.** We do this by using cliche's, talking about other people, changing the subject, even debating ideas. It's all a way to keep people from finding out how vulnerable we feel.

There are two advantages in being a quiet stream kind of person. One is that we build an atmosphere condusive to communication. People will talk to us, feeling that we will listen and actually hear. They will also be more likely to take time to listen to us and hear us, too. Secondly, we will be able to accomplish more, enjoy life more, feel a sense of purpose, and deal successfully with the things that threaten us.

Philippians 4:6-7 shows how we can become "quiet stream" people. First it says, "Be anxious for nothing, . . ." How is that for a direct, open command? How can God tell us not to be anxious? For many people that's like saying, "Don't think!" Anxiety is so much a part of their life that it's almost the same as being awake. But when God tells us not to be anxious, he provides an alternative way to live that will replace our anxiety, and we will become "quiet stream" people.

The alternative is to pray (talk to God) about **every-thing.** " . . . in everything by prayer and supplication with thanksgiving let your requests be made known to God."

WHAT DO YOU THINK?

Looking back over this chapter what change could you make in each area mentioned to affect the way your parents react to you?

1. Pendulum Clock or Self-Winding Watch?

2. Intelligent Quarter Horse or Stubborn Mule?

3. Chattering Brook or Quiet Stream?

ROTATING FAN OR AIR CONDITIONER?

If you have an allergy to pollen you can appreciate the difference between a fan and an air conditioner. A fan is nice to have if an air conditioner is not available. At least it keeps the air moving. But since a fan does not filter the air it moves, whatever is in the air is circulated by the fan, too. An air conditioner is so much better. Not only does it cool the air, it filters the air.

Some people are like fans, the atmosphere around them is polluted, and they don't change it. Pollution comes in, pollution is blown out. It takes little effort, and certainly no creativity to pass on to other people the pollution that comes our way.

How much better it is to be like an air conditioner!

The atmosphere around us is **changed** as we filter it.

Philippians 4:8 gives us a ready-made filter so that we can become air conditioners instead of just fans; "Finally, brethren, whatever is true, whatever is honorable, whatever is right, whatever is pure, whatever is lovely, whatever is of good repute, if there is any excellence and if anything worthy of praise, let your mind dwell on these things." This means forgetting, shoving out of our minds and rejecting things that are false, degrading, immoral, polluted, selfish, and repulsive.

But **how** can we filter out the pollution we don't want and change the atmosphere around us? It takes a conscious effort in two ways. First, we can make an effort to avoid taking in so much pollution. This simply means intelligently avoiding exposure to things that are advertised as degrading, immoral, polluted, selfish, and repulsive. Think about movie advertisements, for instance. It doesn't take too much brain power to figure out the difference between movies that are going to shovel the pollution at you and ones that will not put your filter on "overload."

The second way to filter out pollution and change the atmosphere around us is to make a conscious effort to replace thoughts about pollution that we've been exposed to with thoughts about things in life that are true, honorable, right, pure, lovely, attractive, and excellent. The way to forget the pollution is to think about what God says is good.

WHAT DO YOU THINK?

What are some things that you can think about, instead of the pollution you've been exposed to? In

other words, what are some things you've been exposed to that pass the Philippians 4:8 test? List them here.

Philippians 4:9 tells us how to function as air conditioners. "The things you have learned and received and heard and seen in me, practice these things; and the God of peace shall be with you."

Practice is not only important in football, track, basketball, or any other skill; it is important in living! In sports, the best place to practice is on the field or court. In living, the best place to practice is at home! If we can be successful at building an atmosphere of open, honest, healthy communication at home, we can do it anywhere. What do you say? Is it worth a try? If so, try the ideas in the "What Is Your Plan" section before you go on to the next chapter.

WHAT IS YOUR PLAN?

1. **Decide which of the following you want to work on first, second, third and fourth and number them.**
   ____ **Self-winding watch**
   ____ **Intelligent quarter horse**
   ____ **Quiet stream**
   ____ **Air conditioner**
   There's a practice exercise for each of them here.

Do them in the order you decided above, and practice for several weeks with number one before going on to number two.

SELF-WINDING WATCH

Look through the Psalms and write out on a 3 x 5 card every verse you can find that has the word "joy" in it. Memorize any that are especially significant to you.

INTELLIGENT QUARTER HORSE

For two weeks try doing immediately whatever your folks ask you to do, then listing all the reasons you can think of why they asked you to do it. Make your lists a multiple choice for your parents to check.

QUIET STREAM

In big letters on a 3 x 5 card, write the word "STOP." Then on the other side of the card write out, word for word, Philippians 4:6-7. Be sure to leave the bottom half of the card empty. Then on the left edge of the card, write the days of the week, starting with today. Now keep this card with you at all times and whenever you begin to feel anxious, pull out the card, read the word "STOP" out loud, then turn the card over and read the verse out loud. Keep a tally of how many times you use the card each day. If, by the end of a week, you have to use the card less than at the beginning, that's progress. Prepare another card for another week if you need to.

AIR CONDITIONER

Build a list of things you think about and talk about that pass the Philippians 4:8 test. Keep a sheet or pad of paper next to your bed, and at the end of each day for two weeks go over the things you talked about and thought about during the day. Then thank God for giving them to you.

CHAPTER IV

Recycle Your Relationship

In the last chapter we looked at the atmosphere you created in your relationship with your parents. Now let's turn our attention to some of the games teenagers use to manipulate their parents and what the results of these games are. We'll also look at a passage of Scripture that will help recycle our relationships with our parents.

When you want something (like the use of the car) and your parents won't let you have it, what do you do? Do you get mad? Do you pout, argue, apply pressure, or bargain? What do **you** do to get what you want? How do you handle the situation when all is said and done and you still haven't got what you wanted?

Frustration is something we all have to live with. Some people handle frustration well while others fall apart. People who can't handle frustration are often miserable to be around because frustration is such a large part of any relationship. Maybe if we could be all alone with a surplus of resources we wouldn't have to deal with so much frustration—except the frustration of being lonely. Or maybe if we had the power to control everyone around us we wouldn't have to deal with frustration. But most of us don't have that power so we end up having to deal with our feelings when we get frustrated. We need to look at one very common response to frustration—manipulation.

Manipulation is a way of forcing your parents to give you what you want; so is overpowering, but the difference is that the person who overpowers simply demands, whereas the manipulator doesn't openly demand or even ask for what he or she wants. The biggest problem with manipulation is that we damage our relationship with the person we're manipulating. The teenager who manipulates his or her parents starts with the feeling that a direct request will lead to refusal so he's got to go about it another way.

One writer says "The person who can't be open in asking for what he or she wants is reflecting an inability to be open on sharing any kind of feelings, which constitutes a formidable barrier to healthy relating." [1]

What are some of the manipulating games teenagers play? Let's look at some of them and their results:

Vague—The game of vague is really an excuse-lie. It is a statement like, "I can't make it to Bible study tonight because of my homework." It wouldn't be a manipulative statement if homework were the only reason for staying home. But if you're expecting a phone call from a friend or you simply want to be alone for a while or any of a dozen other reasons is keeping you home, you're manipulating. You figure your parents won't let you stay home for the real reason, so you give them a reason they are likely to accept.

Sure, you'll do some homework and that will make it all right—or will it? You may get to stay home, but you may also make it difficult for your parents to keep trusting you. Other examples of popular times to play "vague" are statements like, "Oh, we'll be back after the ball game." "I'll see if I can mow the lawn on Monday." "Don't worry, I'm doing fine at school."

Suffer—The game of suffer is a way of making parents feel guity for "making you suffer" by frustrating you. Statements such as, "Don't worry about me, I'll find something to do." "Do what you want, I don't care." are manipulative when the fact is that you really do care. If your parents feel guilty for a while, they will probably let you do what you want next time.

Fair play—The game of fair play is another way to use the power of guilt. Statements such as "You get a gift for Jimmy, why not one for me?" appeal to a parent's sense of fair play and equality. It's funny how we only notice the fair play game when the other person has the advantage.

Promised—The game of promised is used when it's to your advantage. "You promised I could have the car tonight, remember?" is not manipulation if it's a reminder of a recent promise. But sometimes we ask for something so far ahead and so casually that we make it seem umimportant. Then when the event comes along we make a big deal of the promise made weeks ago.

Disappointment—The game of disappointment is the one played by expecting something of your parents but not telling them what the expectation is until they've blown it, then getting angry or sad.

When we play disappointment we are saying in effect, "If you were really a good parent you would have read my mind." The game of disappointment is based on a lot of unspoken assumptions like: "Good parents are always available." "Good parents meet all my needs." "Good parents never get angry."

There are many other ways to manipulate. We hope the games mentioned will help you become aware of games you might be using to manipulate your parents. When we manipulate, we treat our parents as objects rather than as persons. This is too bad because we then feel further away from them than before. If our manipulation didn't work we're mad at them for being so stubborn. If it worked we feel like we've put one over on them, and that feeling eats away at our respect for them.

RECYCLING

You can recycle your relationship with your parents, even if it is presently quite rotten. And a recycled relationship with Dad and Mom can become a beautiful, supportive, intimate relationship. Colossians 3:1-17 is a dynamite guide to better relationships in the body of Christ. Let's look at it with parent relationships in mind.

Verse one qualifies the whole chapter. "If then you have been raised up with Christ," shows that the following verses are written to people who have established a personal relationship with Christ. If you haven't established that relationship you will find the rest of the instructions on recycling impossible because the process is based on the power of the Holy Spirit in the lives of people who have started a personal relationship with God. If you're not sure what this is all about, let me suggest you find a friend who is sure and ask. It is a new beginning that will affect all your life.

"If then you have been raised up with Christ, keep seeking the things above, where Christ is, seated at the right hand of God. Set your mind on the things above, not on the things that are on earth." Maybe you have owned a windup watch that runs down and has to be reset periodically. What do you set it by—telephone time, radio time? Standard times for the minds of God's people is "the things above." "The things that are on earth" are the standard for thinking and behavior called normal. "Normal" means how most people think and act. Normal, for many parent-teen relationships, is growing independence, therefore angry confrontation or manipulation, rebellion, indifference, and selfishness. If we set our minds on the things above we will have a different standard of what is normal.

"For you have died and your life is hidden with Christ in God. When Christ, who is our life, is revealed, then you also will be revealed with Him in glory." Verses three and four form a positive basis for a recycled self-image. Did you realize that, from God's perspective, the old you died with Christ on the cross and the new you is hidden with Christ in God Himself. What He is developing as He works in your life, the masterpiece that is you, will finally be unveiled when Christ is revealed in glory. So thank God He is still working on you!

Since from God's perspective we have died and our new life is being formed in Christ we are to "consider the members of your earthly body as dead" to certain things. In other words we are to live like what we are. Salvation is like the recycling process in that God makes new people of us. 2 Corinthians 5:17 says it this way: "Therefore if any man is in Christ, he is a new creature; the old things passed away; behold, new things have come." Colossians 3:5 simply says that we are to act like the new people we are. To start with, we are to consider ourselves "as dead to immorality, impurity, passion, evil desire, and greed, which amounts to idolatry."

WHAT DO YOU THINK?

1. How would you define the list in Colossians 3:5 in your own words? Write your definitions, then check them in a Bible dictionary. Your church library should have one.

2. How will considering yourself dead to the things listed in verse 5 affect your relationship with your parents?

Verse six shows that God thinks about each of the items in verse five, and verse seven shows that they are normal living for people whom Christ has not redeemed. But they are not to be normal behavior for God's people.

PUT OFF

Verse eight lists some things to reject. "But now you also, put them all aside: anger, wrath, malice, slander, and abusive speech from your mouth." If they have been part of our relationship with our parents we are to take off these forms of communication like we would our dirty clothes. That means we avoid making ourselves angry. When we feel anger coming, we recognize it, own it, (rather than blaming it on someone else) then get rid of it. We are to treat wrath, or rage the same way.

Wrath, or rage, is anger that we hold onto, nourish inside us, and build. It may have started as a frustration or hurt when Dad or Mom blocked one of our goals. We got angry, which didn't help the situation but made us feel better. So we built up the rage inside. This is normal behavior for many people, but for God's people, building up wrath is a no-no. Instead we are to put wrath aside. Doing this may be difficult, but it will quickly improve our relationship with our parents if we do.

Malice, slander, and abusive speech are other reactions to frustration and anger. Like wrath and anger they are to be put off. Consider the difference it might make if your pattern of reaction to frustration has been wrath, malice or abusive speech and you begin putting these aside. Your home is going to change!

Verse nine adds another ingredient to the recycling process. "Do not lie to one another . . ." You've probably been told not to lie since you were little. But lying for a teenager is more of a problem than it is for a child. It is important as a teenager to be able to be trusted. When you lie, you lose credibility. Independence is given by parents on the basis of their trust, so it is important to build that trust.

But a more basic reason for putting aside lying is given in verses 9-11. It is who we are—people who have put aside the old self with its evil practices and have put on the new self which is constantly being renewed.

PUT ON

Verse twelve adds to the recycling process by telling us more about ourselves and giving us some things to put on, like new clothes. "And so, as those who have been chosen of God, holy and beloved, put on a heart of compassion, kindness, humility, gentleness and patience." God has chosen us, set us apart and loved us. Therefore we are to act like we are chosen, set apart and loved. This means being compassionate, kind, humble, gentle and patient.

Are you compassionate with your folks? Being compassionate means we can feel as they feel. It's hard to be compassionate when we are trying hard to make them feel what we feel. If we can listen, not worry about winning an argument, avoid withdrawing and trying to hurt our parents when they frustrate us, and avoid the temptation to manipulate, we may be able to understand our folks to the point of being able to feel what they are feeling.

Are you kind to your parents? How about when you both need the car? Kindness sometimes means we don't make an issue of something even when we are right and the other person is wrong. Sometimes kindness means biting our lip instead of saying "See, I told you so!"

Humility means a perspective on ourselves that allows us to put other people first, giving them preferential treatment. Jesus' humility included going all the way to death on a cross with all the humiliation it involved. The King of Glory became our servant. Humility in our family might mean giving preferential treatment to our family members, especially parents, instead of seeking it for ourselves. It might mean choosing to be your parents' servant. Remember this is not normal, it is heavenly; but so are you!

Gentleness and patience go hand in hand. It seems that gentle people are more patient, and patient people find it easier to be gentle. Are you gentle and patient with your parents? Remember, they are human and make mistakes. Sometimes they learn more slowly than you do. After all, you are used to learning. You are probably still in school, they have probably been out of school for a long time. You might get impatient and expect them to make up their minds about something when they're not ready. If you jump all over them when they blow it, you make it even rougher on them. "But," you say, "they certainly are not patient and gentle with me!" Colossians 3 doesn't tell us to be patient and gentle only with the people who are patient and gentle with us. We are to initiate gentleness and patience. We are to put on patience and gentleness regardless of whether others put it on or not.

Verse thirteen adds a couple of ideas that are especially pertinent to parent-teen relationships. "bearing with one another, and forgiving each other, whoever has a complaint against any one; just as the Lord forgave you, so also should you." How did God forgive us? He extended forgiveness before we asked for it. We didn't have to wait for God to decide whether or not to forgive us. Forgiveness is ready for us to grab! That's how we are to forgive. Do you have a complaint about your dad or mom? Are they old-fashioned, naive, perfectionistic, severe, inconsistent, legalistic, you name it? Forgive—you can do it because Jesus forgave you. Then hang in there with a parent who is not perfect. That's what bearing with one another means.

"And beyond all these things put on love, which is the perfect bond of unity." Let's not take love for granted. Build it, decide to love your parents in a new way every week, then practice it all week. This will bring you together eventually, even if your folks resist it for a while.

Verse fifteen gives you an arbiter whenever you're not sure how to respond. Which response, which alternative do you predict will leave you most at peace with God? Choose that one. As the peace of Christ rules in your heart your parents will absorb that peace and be more peaceful themselves.

Three words at the end of verse fifteen act like magic in parent-teen relationships: "and be thankful." Thankfulness is so easy to forget—express it all the time. Don't wait. It seems so insignificant but it is so important.

"Let the word of Christ richly dwell within you . . ." Is God's word something you know or something you live? Does it dwell in your head or in your life?

Verse seventeen sums up the recycling process. "And whatever you do in word or deed, do all in the name of the Lord Jesus, giving thanks through Him to God the Father." This verse sums it up for all week as well as Sunday, for home as well as church, for your relationship with your parents as well as with other Christians. Recycle your relationship and start a new home life!

WHAT IS YOUR PLAN?

1. Which of the items to "put on" grabs you as one

you might try this week? Write it on a 3 x 5 card and carry it around in your pocket or purse. Every time you find a way to exercise this quality, put a 1 on the backside of your card. See how many 1's you'll have by this time next week, and watch the impact it has on your folks.

2. Which of the items to "put off" strike you as most important for you? You might pick up a little book by Norman Wright called An Answer to Anger and Frustration (Harvest House Publishers).

---

1. Jerry Gillies, **Friends** (New York: Coward, McCann, & Geghegan, 1976), p. 118.

CHAPTER V

Problem Parents

As you have been reading, you may have been saying to yourself, "Well that's O.K. for Dave's or Sue's family but it sure won't work in mine. You don't know my parents. I'd like to try some of your suggestions, but they would backfire and only make things worse."

Some parents **are** more open to change than others. Some can handle the changes you're making, others can't. Some are even having problems coping with the changes they are facing as they grow older. But let's be careful not to make excuses or look for someone to blame. Probably every parent is at some time a problem to his or her teenagers. The question is, do we try to control and if we can't control, do we alienate? Can we look for ways to change our approach so that our parents can respond more easily and less defensively to us?

LEARNING TO BE PARENTS

Do you remember what made you a teenager? You turned thirteen. But before being a teenager you were a person, right? Well before your parents were parents they were persons. When they got married they had to get used to the role of husband and wife. Then along you came and they were suddenly parents (if you were the firstborn.) But parenting is not just having babies. Many parents never had any babies. They adopted children. And many couples who had a baby gave it up for adoption. So what is parenting?

The role of parenting, just like most roles, is learned; not formally in a school or church setting, but by imitation and absorption. Parents learn how to be parents by doing the things most natural for them. This usually is one form of what their parents did. Even people who say, "I'm never going to do what my parents did to me," absorb most of their parenting behaviors and attitudes from their parents anyway.

Parents are expected to act like parents. Even divorced parents are expected to maintain an interest in and support of their children. It is the expectation that parents act like parents, that makes parenting a role. When parents get used to playing their role a certain way (usually the way they saw their parents play it), they become comfortable with their role and then tend to avoid changing it. In fact, your parents may continue to interact with you as their child even after you are adult enough to have a family of your own!

What can you do as a teenager if one of your parents or both are "problem parents" for you? Can you change your parents? In a word, NO! DON'T EVEN TRY But you can change the way you respond to your parents; and if you do, they will be likely to change the way they respond to you. It's sort of like a game of chess. If your dad knows how you're going to move your chessman because you always play the game the same way, he doesn't have to change. But if you change your game, he will have to change his in response.

WHAT DO YOU THINK?

1. **What are some habits, practices, behaviors, attitudes etc. you wish your parents would change?**

2. **How do you respond to each of these habits, practices, behaviors, attitudes etc. presently?**

CHANGE THAT ENCOURAGES CHANGE

You affect the behavior of people around you more than you probably realize. The idea that your parents do all the teaching and you do all the learning doesn't account for a lot of parenting behavior. The fact is, children teach their parents many things. For instance, a dad tells his teenage son to be sure to be home by 11:00 p.m. and the son agrees. But 11:00 rolls by, then 11:30 and still no word. At 11:45 the son bounces in, says "hi" to his parents and walks to his room. When his dad reminds him he is 45 minutes late he makes a casual remark about forgetting to look at the clock and apologizes. His parents accept the apology and let it go. But what else is happening? **The teenager is teaching his parents not to trust him.** If this teenager changed his behavior, let's say to calling his folks before 11:00 p.m. if he saw he wasn't going to make the deadline, his parents might be learning to trust him more.

When you find yourself having a problem with one of your parents you can do one of three things:

1) **Blame your parents.** This is the most popular response to a parent-teen problem. Of course parents reciprocate—they blame you. And what has been solved? It gets down to who has the last word, and that usually means you lose, right? "If Dad wasn't so old-fashioned, I'd be able to make friends much more easily. But he even insists on meeting my dates—the word gets around and they are scared off." So you fight the problem by fighting your parents hoping that after a while they will lose patience and let you do it your way. But maybe not.

2) **Give up and get out.** Some teenagers blame themselves for their problems instead of blaming their parents. This is both good news and bad news. The bad news, first, is that after they blame themselves they escape, either physically by finding a way to leave home, or relationally by just not associating with their parents and not communicating with them any more. The good news is that by blaming themselves, teenagers who take this option are admitting that they own the problems. At least when they own the problem, these teenagers are just a few steps away from solving it.

3) **Look for a way to change.** If you take this option you are not casting blame on your parents, nor are you casting it on yourself. It is less important to find out who is to blame than it is to get the problem solved. Since doing what you've been doing hasn't solved the problem, changing to do something different might work. Of course the change you pick might not work but the chance that it might is better than the certainty that what you've been doing won't work, isn't it?

If you wait for your parents to change you are

forced to live with the problem as it is until they change. Wouldn't it be better to choose how you want to change, then let them respond?

For instance, Sharon has a problem with her parents. Her dad insists on meeting everybody she goes out with. If she chooses the first option, she blames her dad for not having enough dates. She figures he is making her unpopular. This doesn't change anything! She doesn't get any more dates, and she just has a war going on with her dad. If she chooses the second option, she gives up on dating until she can leave home, or else she has secret "dates" that her dad doesn't know about. She probably has to lie a lot and her dates aren't as much fun as they could be if they were "up front." If she chooses the third option she looks for some alternatives. Maybe **she** insists on introducing her dates to her dad without telling them it's one of his rules. Maybe she finds that her dad wasn't scaring boys off after all. She was. Maybe she finds some other alternatives. The important thing is that she looks for a way to change.

There are some areas in relationships, including parent-teen relationships where a change you make is quite likely to encourage change in your parents. Let's see if we can get a handle on these areas.

CHANGE YOUR REWARD

You reward your parents for many of the ways they behave toward you. So they keep behaving that way. For instance, parents who are overprotective are rewarded for their overprotectiveness. It takes a lot of effort to be overprotective—your parents won't expend all that energy unless there's something in it for them. Your question, then, is what are they getting out of being overprotective? How am I rewarding them? How can I change my reward?

If your parents are overprotective you might find that they need to feel needed. Maybe you have made so many giant strides towards independence lately that your parents are feeling rather useless. So they respond by becoming overprotective, and your reaction has been to assert your independence even more. Your assertion of independence is rewarding their need to be overprotective because the more you assert your independence the more they feel the need to protect you from making the mistakes they know come with new independence!

If you changed your response to your parents' overprotectiveness to one of asserting your interdependence with them, finding ways to let them feel needed, they would be likely to let up on you. You will have changed their reward. Instead of rewarding their need to feel needed, you reward their dependence upon you and their investment in you. By asserting your interdependence with them you reward their love, not their need to control.

PLUG THE FUEL LINE

Sometimes you can't think of another reward to change to, so you have to respond to your folks with another kind of change. Something you are doing is fueling the problem, making it worse. If you can figure out what it is and cut off the fuel to the problem, it will go away. That is what we mean by plugging the fuel line. The problem won't really be solved, it will just disappear for lack of energy.

For instance, what if your folks are legalistic?

We're not talking about families with rules and covenants. Family rules and covenants are worked out together, understood and agreed to by all. By legalistic parents we mean parents who appeal to a set of rules, a code, or some outside authority to make all the decisions for them. Legalistic parents are so concerned about making "right" decisions that they get very uptight when they run across a situation where there's no rule already written.

For instance, maybe your attitude toward your church is negative. You may have a lot of very good reasons for being negative about your church, but think about what a change in attitude might accomplish. Your folks might just relax, feeling confident that you're not "straying from the faith." You may be able to develop communication about decisions, rather than quickly establishing fixed defensive positions. Your parents may even come to the point of being negotiable on issues they felt previously they could not "compromise." So a change in attitude might help both you and your parents!

Another example might be if you notice that your parents are quite argumentative. It seems that every time you disagree with them a long argument begins. What could be fueling their need to argue? Can you plug the fuel line? As with the tango, it takes two (or more) to argue. Maybe you are fueling the argument. The more you try to change your parents or their decisions the more they resist you and argue. So plug the fuel line and stop arguing. Change your position. The inflexible position of arguing that you are right only fuels the argument. Change your position and watch your parents respond by changing theirs. You may not get your way but chances are both you and your parents will be happier with what you come up with together.

CHANGE YOUR SIGNALS

A third change that you might be able to make that will encourage change in your parents is in the signals you are giving them. We all respond to signals, especially when driving our cars. A red light means stop, a yellow sign with the letters "XING" means there's a crossing ahead, etc. We all give signals to each other, too. Stomping around the house with a frown on your face usually means, "I'm in a bad mood, don't cross me or I'll bite off your head." We send signals with our expressions, our actions, our words, our gestures, even our dress and appearance.

Think about your parents' reactions to you. Do they tend to respond a certain way rather consistently? For instance, when you are feeling tired and bored do they come on strong and accuse you of being lazy? If you get defensive and angry about their reaction, things will tend to get worse. Instead, think abut the signals they could be picking up. They might be feeling that you don't care about them or about your chores. Maybe they are getting rejection signals from you. Maybe they are getting signals that you are feeling angry and non-cooperative.

Whether the signals they are receiving are accurate or not is less important than that you change the signals. When you do, they will probably change their reaction. You might do or say something that lets them know you appreciate them, for instance. You might try encouraging them in whatever they are doing. You might simply ask them what they are doing. It will signal to them that you're interested in them.

WHO IS THE PROBLEM?

When it comes to reality, problem parents are really a challenge to creativity. You can think of problem parents as a block to your growth and independence if you wish, but that won't help. Trying to change your parents won't help either. It will simply encourage them to become more set in their ways.

So rather than trying to change your parents or giving up and getting out, take the time to think about some alternatives. If you do you will find that even extreme parents become easier to communicate with and easier to live with.

WHAT IS YOUR PLAN?

1. I could change rewards by _____

2. I could plug the fuel line by_____

3. I could change the following signals_____

CHAPTER VI

Put On Your Headphones

When you want to go beyond just hearing, to really listening to a favorite record, you put on your headphones, right? Other sounds are blocked out, it seems like the sound is in the middle of your head.

Jesus said, "He who has ears to hear, let him be listening, and consider and perceive and comprehend by hearing." Three times in the Gospel of Matthew Jesus made this statement (11:15, 13:9, 43, AMP). You and I are called to be listeners.

There are hundreds of verses in the Bible that talk about hearing or being heard. The Psalms reflect the listening and the hearing qualities of God. Psalm 34:15 and 17 say, "The eyes of the Lord are toward the righteous, and His ears are open to their cry . . . the righteous cry for help, the Lord hears and delivers them out of all their distress and troubles" (AMP).

WHAT DO YOU THINK?

1. How would you define listening?

2. How would you describe your listening ability?

3. How would your parents describe your listening ability?

Did you know that:

One of the greatest complaints of parents is that their teenagers don't listen to them.

Most people do not really know what is meant by listening nor have many people received any training to become better listeners.

The Bible commands us to be ready listeners.

When communication breaks down because somebody isn't listening we not only limit our relationship with each other, but our fellowship suffers and we stifle our own growth as Christians.

TOTAL LISTENING

No one can accurately estimate the value of listening or being listened to. As teenagers one of the greatest gifts we can give to our parents is total listening. Paul Tournier put it this way: "How beautiful, how grand and liberating this experience is, when people learn to help each other. It is impossible to overemphasize the immense need humans have to be really listened to. Listen to all the conversations of our world, between nations as well as those between couples. They are for the most part, dialogues of the deaf." [1]

"By consistently listening to a speaker, you are conveying the idea: 'I'm interested in you as a person, and I think that what you feel is important. I respect your thoughts, and even if I don't agree with them, I know that they are valid for you. I feel sure that you have a contribution to make. I'm not trying to change or evaluate you. I just want to understand you. I think you're worth listening to, and I want you to know that I'm the kind of person that you can talk to.' " [2]

The Living Bible expresses these thoughts about listening: "What a shame—yes, how stupid!—to decide before knowing the facts" (Proverbs 18:13). "Any story sounds true until someone tells the other side and sets the record straight" (Proverbs 18:17). "The wise man learns by listening; the simpleton can learn only by seeing scorners punished" (Proverbs 21:11).

What is listening? **When we are listening to another person we are not thinking about what we are going to say when he stops talking.** We are concentrating on what he is saying.

Have you ever had so many thoughts running around in your head while your dad or mom was talking that your head felt ready to explode? Have you ever thought that you knew what your dad or mom was going to say and you finished the statement or question for them? Communication doesn't depend on our answering for the other person. Nor do we really have to respond as quickly as we often do. In fact our responses will usually sound much wiser if we patiently absorb what Dad or Mom is saying; then think about our response, then respond.

Interrupting a person is one way of showing that we are not really listening. Sometimes we interrupt verbally, and sometimes we interrupt nonverbally. Often the nonverbal interruptions are the most annoying. The impatient look, the sigh, glancing around the room, crossing the arms, drumming fingers on the chair or table—all these and other mannerisms are ways of saying, "Are you through? I'm not really listening and I want to talk." One way we can let parents know we are really tuned in is to listen with our bodies. For instance, how do you listen with your hands? When your parents are talking to you are your hands:

Playing with something they are holding?

Turning the pages of a book or magazine?

Twittling thumbs?

We can let a person know that we are ready and willing to be a listener by stopping what we are doing and turning to him with our ears, our eyes, and the rest of our body. This is part of total listening.

COMPLETE ACCEPTANCE

Total listening is not only concentrating on what the other person is saying. **Listening means we completely accept what is being shared without judging what is said or how it is stated.**

Often we fail to hear a message because we don't like the words that are used or the other person's tone of voice. If you feel sometimes that your parents are being unfair, arbitrary, unreasonable, dogmatic or traditional, you're not alone. It's hard to listen when your parents are unreasonable, isn't it; but it is possible. Acceptance does **not** mean that you have to agree with everything your dad or mom is saying. By acceptance we mean that you understand that what is being shared is what the other person believes or feels. Your dad or mom is sharing part of his or her life with you. This does not mean that you have to feel or believe the way the other person does. Nor do you even have to agree!

Acceptance does not mean agreement. There is an important difference between them. If you were agreeing you might say something like, ''You are right. The way you understand the situation is realistic and correct. I misunderstood, and that's why I disagreed. But now I understand and agree." If you were accepting, even though you might not agree, you might say something like, "I'm not sure I can agree with all you've said, but I'm glad you shared it with me. I'm sure we can continue to discuss it. I care about you as a person and I hope you know I care even though we don't see eye to eye."

Often parents and teenagers continue to misunderstand each other because both are trying very hard to be understood rather than to understand. You can avoid a lot of long uncomfortable hassles if you do your best to understand **before** you attempt to be understood. Notice we said "before," not "instead of." Here is how to make sure you understand and at the same time give your dad or mom the feeling that you understand: When your dad or mom says something, say it back to them in your own words. If they feel that you understood them they will confirm your paraphrase; if not, they will correct it. Continue doing this until they make a feeling statement.

For instance, your dad says, "Son, I think you've been spending entirely too much time with your girlfriend lately." Instead of agreeing or disagreeing try to understand what is behind his statement—what he's feeling. You say, "You think Sue and I have been seeing too much of each other." If this is what he thinks, your father will expand or clarify his thinking with something like, "You don't seem to have time to get your chores done and I never see you doing homework any more." You could object and defend yourself, but wait. Paraphrase again. "I've messed up on some of my responsibilities and you're worried about my grades?" Your dad will now probably be more specific. "Well the lawn didn't get

mowed Saturday and the garage is still a mess."
Now you have an idea about the source of your dad's
first comment, but reflect again. "The lawn looks
shaggy quickly at this time of year." Maybe at this
point your dad will tell you how he feels. "When the
house is messy, it makes me feel like a slob." Of
course, you and I know that no house can **make** your
dad feel anything. But the important thing is that he
has let you know how he feels. At this point avoid
suggestions, just see if you can do something to help
him feel better. For instance you might just walk out
and sweep the garage, mow the lawn, or maybe even
just straighten up the room you are in.

Does acceptance mean you cannot express your
opinion? No, your opinions and judgments are
important. But if you wait to express your opinions
until **after** you have listened, you will avoid much
misunderstanding and conflict. You will also avoid
many foolish mistakes.

FULL UNDERSTANDING

If we have truly listened, we will be able to feel the
feeling the other person is feeling. The other person
feels he has been listened to and he responds by
feeling understood, respected and loved. This is
satisfying to most people. Its opposite—the feeling of
being misunderstood, not respected or loved—moti-
vates most people to continue griping, hassling,
blaming, placating or judging until they feel more
satisfied.

Hearing is not enough! You can hear without really
listening. In listening it is not enough to be able to
repeat the words of the other person. We have to
know what those words mean to the other person.

Hearing is mostly concerned with information while listening concerns itself with persons. When you listen, you show you care about the other person. Hearing is usually for our own sake while listening is for the other person's sake.

WHAT DO YOU THINK?

Let's test your listening ability. Be sure you answer these questions only for yourself without evaluating how your parents would respond. After you've answered them you may want to ask your folks how they think you answered and if your answer was accurate.

1. What do I assume about my parents when they talk to me?

2. What do I think about when my parents are talking?

3. How can I tell nonverbally that my parents are listening to me? How can they tell if I'm listening to them?

4. What words or verbal responses do I use to let my folks know I'm listening?

5. When I don't want to listen I:

6. When my dad or mom really listens to me I feel:

DERAILING THE LISTENING PROCESS

Often we start listening then go off the listening track and start doing something else. Sometimes we get derailed before we've even started listening. Here's how.

Sometimes we don't care enough about our parents to want to know what is going on in their lives. Listening is a form of loving and caring. In fact, listening is one of the ways God expresses His love for us. He wants us to pray because He really listens.

Sometimes we don't listen because our parents are expressing things we don't want to hear. Their words upset and convict us, so we tune them out or jam their frequency. This tuning-out process is called ''being narrow-minded.'' Sometimes teenagers are more narrow-minded than their parents!

Sometimes we derail the listening process by letting our mind wander while the other person is talking. We are capable of listening five times as fast as we can speak. If you can listen at 400 words a minute and your dad is speaking at 120 words a minute, what is you mind doing with the rest of that time? **Listening** takes self-discipline to continue focusing on what is being said.

Sometimes listening is derailed by the relationship

of communication. Specialists tell us that there are six messages in communications:

1. What your folks mean to say;
2. What they actually say;
3. What you hear;
4. What you think you hear;
5. What you say about what your folks said;
6. What your folks think you said about what they said.

This relationship is further complicated by what is called ''mixed messages.'' These are the situations where your folks say one thing with their words but where their tone of voice or body language say something quite different. You probably do this too, sometimes.

INCREASING YOUR LISTENING ABILITY

Do you **want** to listen better? If you really want to listen you have already taken a giant step in increasing your listening ability. Keep your motivation going by counting the things you learn about your friends and family each time you finish talking with them.

Secondly, avoid interrupting, like you would the plague. Concentrate on what your dad or mom is saying. Try to create an atmosphere for communication. You can do this by stopping whatever else you've been doing and facing your dad or mom. Then, if possible, sit down or lean on something—this communicates nonverbally that you are waiting for him to say something. When he does, reflect by paraphrasing his idea. Then let him talk at his own pace.

WHAT IS YOUR PLAN?

1. Please list three specific behaviors you will either change or begin, during this next week, to improve your listening ability.

   1. _____

   2. _____

   3. _____

2. What will a pattern of better listening do for you as a person?

3. Memorize Proverbs 18:13 and James 1:19.

---

1. Paul Tournier, **To Understand Each Other** (Richmond, Va.: John Knox Press, 1967), p. 29.
2. George E. & Nikki Koehler, **My Family: How Shall I Live With It?** (Chicago: Rand McNally & Co. 1968), p. 57.

CHAPTER VII

Different Stations

If radios had personalities of their own, can you imagine how they would feel? Some would probably feel quite important as a constant companion to their owners and always "turned-on." But others, like those in a lot of stores, might feel very frustrated and lonely because even though they are playing much of the time, nobody's listening! Do you ever feel like a store radio—talking and expressing yourself only to discover that nobody is listening? Are your messages getting through? In one survey parents listed lack of effective communication as the third main cause of tension between them and their teenagers. The teenagers, however, listed inability to communicate with parents as their number one cause of tension.

If I were a radio with a personality of my own and I discovered that nobody was listening to me I think I would change my dial to another station. If I did this enough times I'll bet I'd find a station that people would listen to. Then I'd feel less frustrated and more important. I'm not a radio, but I do find sometimes that I need to "change my station" so people will listen to me. How about you?

WHAT DO YOU THINK?

1. Please rate the communication between yourself and your parents on this scale, 0 being the worst and 10 the best. Circle the number that best describes it.

   0   1   2   3   4   5   6   7   8   9   10

2. Now put a "D" above the number your dad would circle and an "M" above the number your mom would circle.

SAY WHAT YOU THINK

Where does communication begin? What we say is simply a reflection of what we have been thinking and feeling. If you're angry and feel your parents have been unfair, your communication will be different in word, tone of voice and body language than if you're happy with a gift your parents just gave you. Maybe we need to start thinking about what we're thinking about.

Jesus said, "Listen, and understand this thoroughly! It is not what goes into a man's mouth that makes him common or unclean. It is what comes out of a man's mouth that makes him unclean" (Matthew 15:10-12, PHIL).

Maybe you're communicating quite well—your words accurately convey what's going on inside. If this is true and your words are creating problems with your parents, think about your attitudes, your values, your emotions and your ideas. Do they flow with Scripture or buck against it?

WHAT DO YOU THINK?

1. List 10 of your most common attitudes, emotions and your most important values or ideas.

    1.

    2.

    3.

    4.

    5.

    6.

    7.

    8.

    9.

    10.

2. What does the Bible have to say about each of the items you listed? See if you can find several passages that speak to each one. You might get help from your parents, Sunday School teacher, youth minister or pastor, if you have a problem finding the passages.

Sometimes the problem is not in what we are thinking and feeling but in the words we choose to express ourselves. James Fairfield writes, "When you speak, your meaning or intention is in your mind and only partially expressed in your words. At best, your words only sketch a picture of what you mean. At worst, what you say projects the wrong picture entirely and your meaning is lost.

"Yet we persist in believing that words in themselves hold all meaning, and all that is necessary is to look in a dictionary, check the definition listed, and we shall know exactly what the person meant who used the word. We forget that dictionaries merely collect common meanings that people give to words.

"But words do not 'mean' . . . When you speak to me, I can only infer what you mean; I cannot be certain unless I check my inferences with you. And this may take a little more time than we're used to giving." [1]

Many parents complain that two different languages are spoken in their homes—their own and their teenagers! Sometimes they even ask youth ministers to be translators! Some of this may be on purpose. Both parents and teenagers use words with their own meanings to mask what they're really saying.

Meanings are often in people rather than in words. Let's put it this way:

If meanings are in words:	**If meanings are in people:**
If you have the same vocabulary, the message means the same for you and your parents.	You and your parents will not always have exactly the same meaning for what has been said.

The listener is most responsible for the success of communication as he has to decide the words.	Main responsibility for the success of communication lies with the speaker, secondly the listener.
If an error in communication occurs, the problem lies with the hearer.	If an error in communication occurs, the problem belongs to both speaker and hearer.
Feedback is not important.	Feedback is important.
Communication breakdown justifies blame.	Communication breakdown can be repaired by increased awareness and feedback.
When there are differences, one person is right and one is wrong.	There are several meanings possible, therefore more opportunities for solutions. [2]

It is important that our messages are true to our meaning so we can understand and be understood. The Word of God says we are to "speak the truth in love" (Eph. 4:15). To make sure that your messages mean what you want them to mean check your tone of voice and your nonverbal behavior. Do they agree with what you say? The words "Thanks for dinner, Mom," are usually appreciated if said directly to Mom and followed by a kiss than if shouted on the way out the front door.

COMMUNICATING

Saying what we mean is the beginning, but not the whole process of communication. Communication means that we are sharing ourselves both verbally and nonverbally in such a way that the other person can both accept and understand what we mean and intend. In the last chapter we stressed the importance of listening so that communication can take place. In this chapter we hope to help you make it easier for other people, including your parents, to listen to you.

The book of Proverbs is an excellent place to start in the improvement of communication. You might try reading Proverbs from the beginning and every time you find a verse on communication take a 3 x 5 card and write the following items: 1) Reference; 2) Theme; 3) The verse itself in your own words; 4) The result of this type of speech. For instance:

1. Proverbs 4:24.
2. False, willful and contrary talk.
3. Throw away a deceitful mouth with the rest of the trash and avoid tricky talk.
4. Better life and health (v. 22)

After you have all your cards written up, try categorizing them. You might use headings such as "think before you speak," "talking too much," "nagging" etc.

Assuming responsibility for your communication is a second important step. The Bible has lots to say about word power in both the Old and New Testaments. Your words can give your parents a lift or create a burden. They can wound or heal, soothe or rip, produce trust or suspicion, fan both love and hate.

Do you deny responsibility for communication when you feel threatened or angry? Many teenagers do this. When they are angry they say whatever comes to mind. Then when the anger has subsided they say "Well I didn't really mean that, I was angry at the time. Don't believe what I say when I'm mad." The effect of this kind of irresponsibility is that they lose credibility even when they are not angry. Also, people who don't understand their pattern are alienated.

A third step in improving communciation is to speak for yourself rather than for others. When you speak for yourself you tend to avoid sweeping generalizations and speaking for others. Both these habits are resented, even by people who use them themselves. You tend to send "I" messages rather than "you" messages when you speak for yourself. This has the benefit of letting people know what you think or feel without implying that you know and disapprove of what they think or feel.

An "I message" is distinguished from a "you message" in that the speaker claims the problem as his own. A true "I message" has three parts: the feeling, the situation, and how it affects the person speaking. It is a statement of fact rather than an evaluation of the other person. This type of communication is honest and open.

Documenting what you say with descriptive behavioral data aids communication. In other words, when you make a "you" statement to someone like, "you look happy," let them know which of their behaviors led you to the comment you made. For instance, to a comment like "You look happy," you might add, "you're whistling and grinning—what's goin' on?"

Documenting like this is important because it let's other people know the effect of their behavior on you. It also increases your own understanding of yourself by giving you a better idea of how you arrived at your own thoughts and feelings.

A fifth way to improve communication is to tell people how you feel. This is sometimes risky because some people cannot accept feeling statements. The reason for this usually is that when people make feeling statements they think of themselves as weak or inadequate. The stereotype is that strong men and women don't let their emotions show. But there's a difference between denying our emotions and controlling. We can control our emotions much more easily if we tell people how we feel. Making feeling statements also defuses our emotions enough that we don't feel the need to act them out.

For instance, the teenager who says, "Dad, I feel angry and frustrated when I ask for something and you reject my request out of hand," is far ahead of the one who stomps out of the room, grumbling, and ruins the rest of the evening for himself by nursing bad feelings.

Making intention statements is a way of expressing clearly your immediate goals. Intention statements provide others with information about yourself, giving them an idea of what you're willing to do.

Teenager: "I'm planning on spending Tuesday evening at Jane's home. I've been invited for dinner."
Dad: "Haven't you already promised to help your sister with her homework?"
Teenager: "Yes, I'm coming home early to do that. We'll be finished well before dinnertime."
Mom: "I'd like us to sit down together and plan our summer vacation pretty soon."
Teenager: "I'd like that. Usually I don't have any

voice in our vacation plans, and I have some ideas I'd like to share, too."

WHAT DO YOU THINK?

1. See if you can change these "trigger messages" (because they are likely to trigger an argument) into better communication.

Trigger Messages	Better Communication
a. You turkey, don't you know you're supposed to knock before coming into my room?	
b. You embarrassed me thoroughly in front of my boyfriend, and you did it on purpose. I hate you!	
c. You've been in my room again poking around in my things. You don't trust me, do you.	
d. You sure look grumpy today.	
e. You make me so angry!	
f. (After buying the tickets) I was thinking of going to the ball game tomorrow, Dad.	

Sometimes you feel like yelling at your folks, picking an argument, so that your parents realize you're serious. But if you go ahead and act out your feelings you are likely to do at least two things you'll wish you hadn't done. First, you'll focus your parents' attention on the acting out of your feelings. Now they not only have to deal with the issue that got your feelings going, they have to deal with your attitude as well. What's the result? In your parents' eyes the solving of your "attitude problem" becomes most important and everything else, including what you want, becomes secondary.

Second, venting your feelings on your parents slowly teaches them to not bother with you until you get mad. Maybe you would rather they leave you alone most of the time, but if you allow them to invest time and communication in you, your rewards will be many. Most parents want to love their kids, they just need to be told how.

WHAT DO YOU THINK?

1. Have you taught your parents to take you seriously only when you're angry? If so, you need to avoid outbursts of anger.
2. Have you told your parents how you like them to love you? They might express their love more appropriately if you told them how.

THREE "ATIONS" TO AVOID

Accusations are almost always responded to with defensiveness. "You did such and such!" is the accusation and the reflex reaction is "I did not!" When accused and put into a defensive position most people, including parents, see themselves as having to win or lose. Nobody likes to lose, and most parents hate to lose to their teenagers, no matter who is right. So avoiding accusations will allow more productive communication to take place. Secondly, accusations are usually critical and judgmental, and nobody likes to be criticized or judged. Confrontation can occur without accusation if you practice and use the six principles for building communication mentioned in this chapter.

Generalizations are rarely true, and in an argument, they usually confuse the issue. They are most often used to turn an argument into a quarrel. Statements like, "You always . . ." and "you never . . ." lead the argument away from the issues and into comments about each other's personality. You will communicate more successfully if you avoid making generalizations and ignore the generalizations other people make.

Rationalizations are reasons we come up with for our behavior that we think will satisfy other people. For instance Dad says, "Why are you hassling your sister?" Instead of saying "I was feeling ornery and revengeful," you rationalize with "She's been embarrassing me and my girlfriend for the past two weeks." When you rationalize your behavior you invite other people to try to cut you down to size. People start wanting to prove you're not perfect. It's usually better to accept the fact that you're not perfect than to rationalize. Sometimes no response is better than an excuse. Other times admitting immaturity is the best way to learn maturity.

In summary, Paul says a big mouthful about communication in Colossians 4:6 "Let your conversation be gracious as well as sensible, for then you will have the right answer for everyone'' (TLB). Does what you say pass the grace test as well as being sensible? If we tried as hard to be gracious as we do to be sensible or understood, our family communication would be less violent, more loving and more productive.

WHAT IS YOUR PLAN?

1. Circle the phrase you feel best describes the quality of communication in your family:
   a. needs no improvement
   b. highly effective
   c. satisfactory
   d. inconsistent
   e. superficial
   f. frustrating
   g. highly inadequate
2. Now go back and underline the phrases you think your parents would choose.
3. List three things you can do to improve communication with your parents.
   a. _____

   b. _____

   c. _____

4. See if you can set up an ''appointment'' or a date with your dad and then your mom to discuss your communication and your plan to improve it. Take this book along and review the chapter subheads with them.

---

1. James G.T. Fairfield,**When You Don't Agree** (Scottdale, PA.: Herald Press,1977), p. 60.
2. Adapted from Sherod Miller, Elam W. Hunnally and Daniel B. Wackman, **Alive and Aware** (Minneapolis, MN.: Inter-personal Communication Programs), 1975, pp. 153-154.

CHAPTER VIII

Constructive Creative Conflict

You've been promised the use of the car. You've even taken the time to wash it and clean it out because you are taking a girl to the football game tonight. It is your first date with her, and you're doubling with two of her friends. At 5:30 your dad tells you he has to have the car this evening. He's sorry, he promised it to you, but this is an emergency.

WHAT DO YOU THINK?

1. What would you <u>say or do</u> in the situation described? Write down your response.

2. Respond to the paragraph above by writing down how you would <u>feel</u> if your Dad or Mom revoked the car as in the paragraph above.

Is conflict common around your home? If so, you're not alone. Whether lots or just a little, there's conflict in every home. The question is how do we deal with conflict—how do you deal with it in your home? It can be a shattering, disastrous experience, but it can also be constructive and creative. Conflict can drive a wedge between you and your family or, believe it or not, conflict can bring you closer together.

What is conflict? Webster's dictionary defines it as 1) disagreement, emotional tension resulting from incompatible inner needs or drives; 2) war, battle; 3) collision; 4) the opposition of persons or forces that gives rise to the dramatic action in a drama or fiction.

People experience conflict differently. Some are highly threatened at even the hint of conflict. Others find a certain joy in conflict, like the ''Hell's Angel'' who boasts that he's a man of peace—but between periods of peace he enjoys a good fight. Some people win most of the conflict situations they enter, others mostly lose. With other people it's as the saying goes, ''You win some, you lose some.''

Why does conflict occur? The answer is that God made each of us uniquely different. We have different values, feelings, attitudes, ideas and beliefs, and that's perfectly natural. The world would be a rather boring place without differences, don't you think? After all, who would you want to be a xerox copy of? I certainly wouldn't want everybody to be just like me!

Parents sometimes act as if they want you to be just like them, right? Teenagers sometimes act as if they want their parents to be just like them, too. It goes both ways and that's conflict.

When parents and other people can't see things the way we do, we ask what's wrong with them. Obviously they don't understand us or they would agree with us. But once in a while we find out that they did understand us, and they still disagreed. To be misunderstood is threatening; but to be understood and disagreed with can be frightening! We might have to change. So sometimes conflict occurs because of misunderstanding, and sometimes because of disagreement.

Another reason for conflict is spelled out in James 4:1-3. "What causes conflicts and quarrels among you? Do they not spring from the aggressiveness of your bodily desires? You want something which you cannot have, and so you are bent on murder; you are envious, and cannot attain your ambition, and so you quarrel and fight. You do not get what you want, because you do not pray for it. Or, if you do, your requests are not granted because you pray from wrong motives" (NEB). The Bible puts it straight, doesn't it? It says conflicts arise when we don't get our own way.

WHAT DO YOU THINK?

1. **Remember the conflict over the car at the beginning of the chapter? Why did it occur? Check the answer you like best, or add your own.**

    _____a. **The parent and teenager had different values, ideas, beliefs.**

    _____b. **The parent and teenager didn't understand each other.**

    _____c. **The teenager wasn't enough like his parents.**

    _____d. **The parents weren't enough like their teenager.**

    _____e. **Both parent and teenager wanted the car badly, the parent got the car, the teenager got frustrated and resentful.**

    _____f. **Your own reason:** _____

---

2. In a recent conflict with one or both of your parents which of the above were reasons the conflict arose?

3. What did the conflict accomplish, good or bad?

4. How would your dad or mom describe the conflict.

HOW TO CONSTRUCT CREATIVE CONFLICT

Conflict with your parents can build your relationship with them, help you grow, help them grow, and develop your love for each other. But to do these things you may have to give up destructive conflict and construct creative conflict. Here's how:

1. **Argue, don't quarrel.** The important difference between arguing and quarreling is that in arguing you disagree with each other, try to convince each other of your own point of view, and you may even get quite emotional about it, but you don't attack the other person, his motives, or his competence. You don't cut him down. When people quarrel, they try to make the other person feel dumb, stupid or insignificant. They attack the person and attempt to cut him down. The result is that the conquered person either becomes discouraged, depressed and not fun to be with, or he becomes vengeful, planning when he will get even.

When we argue we treat the other person as a person. He may be disagreeable, we may think he is wrong, but we still value him as a person. When we quarrel we treat the other person as an object—an inferior person or a nonperson. We forget his value, which is so high that God sent Jesus to die for him.

2. **Serve, don't demand.** Jesus was constantly in conflict situations when He was physically on earth. In fact His whole lifestyle was in conflict with His culture. But Jesus came to serve—to fulfill the needs of the people He conflicted with. Conflict should tip you off that some people (maybe including yourself) are attempting to fulfill their needs. Have you anticipated and discovered your parents' needs? Can you figure out how to fulfill those needs?

For instance, you're dressed and ready to go with your parents to church. Your Dad walks in, takes a look at you and says, "Come on, it's almost time to go and you're not dressed yet—get a move on." You answer that you are dressed and he explodes. You can't understand his explosion because you've worn those same clothes to church before and he didn't notice, so why the hassle this time? What could some of your Dad's needs be?

This conflict may be due to the fact that both you and your dad are trying to fulfill your own needs. If it's no big thing for you and you immediately go to your room and change, then your needs are not an issue in this confrontation, just your dad's. If you need to be "in" and the clothes your dad wants you to wear are "out" for church activities, the issue becomes your needs versus his.

If you serve your dad and mom rather than demanding that they serve you, you will avoid a lot of common conflict issues. This doesn't mean that you won't have any more conflicts. It does mean you will avoid a lot of hassle over many of the more insignificant problems that somehow spark "forest fires."

3. **Be both agreeable and disagreeable.** "Agreeable" means "able to agree." One of the marks of a maturing person is that he is able to agree. Sometimes we have disagreed so long over so many issues that we take the position that there's a "generation gap" and we can't agree with anything the other side thinks or it will mean we've copped out. The way we can grow is to realize our parents are people—individuals, not symbols of another era. If we can treat them as persons rather than as emissaries from another age we will be "agreeable."

We need to be disagreeable as well as agreeable. This does not mean we should have a disagreeable attitude. But we should be able to disagree. We can learn to disagree without quarreling and overwhelming the other person. We can also learn to disagree without automatically yielding or withdrawing. Being able to disagree is an art that must be learned if conflict is going to be constructive and creative.

CHOOSE YOUR WEAPONS

How you deal with conflict is really far more important than whether your argument is right or wrong. One psychologist suggests that you have five choices in dealing with conflict. Four of them are inadequate and the fifth is constructive and creative. We will call these choices your weapons.

Win—When conflict comes your weapon may be to win. That's right, your weapon is winning in conflict, especially in conflict with your parents. The goal of the "win" weapon is to feel good, to feel powerful, to have your own way, to reinforce your self-image, etc., no matter what the cost.

If this is your weapon, remember when you use it that you have chosen to use it. Like any weapon you choose to use, you are responsible for the damage it does, and the "win" weapon is particularly devastating. When you use the "win" weapon your actions say that your feelings, your own way or plan, or your self-image are more important than the person you are in conflict with. In other words your relationship is less important than your goals.

Withdraw—A second weapon that many people use in conflict is to withdraw. This is an effective weapon when you want to frustrate the person you are in conflict with. People withdraw by leaving the scene, by not talking, by changing the subject, by making wisecracks. The goal of the "withdraw" weapon is to keep things as they are, avoid change, avoid the pain of losing and at the same time avoid the work of winning.

The "withdraw" weapon also says "you're not important to me. And it usually just prolongs the conflict until any solution seems impossible except the traditional one or the one "everyone else is doing."

Compromise—A third weapon for conflict is to compromise. This is when you "give a little to get a little." This is sometimes helpful but often a weapon because we negotiate from the goal of self-interest rather than from the goal of mutual interest. Our fear is that if we take a moderate position and our parents take an extreme position and we both give up the same amount, we end up closer to their position than we would be if we took an extreme position. So "compromise" is a weapon that tends to force people apart rather than together. It also builds mistrust rather than trust, and usually both parties feel they've given up too much.

Yield—A weapon some people won't even consider but others use very effectively is the "yield" weapon. "Give in to get along" is the motto. The person who uses it forces all the responsibility for a decision on the other person. Sometimes it is important to be able to yield. But if you always yield you build a relationship of dependency upon the other person. One-way dependency like this is not nearly as healthy as an interdependent relationship because you become a burden to the other person.

Sometimes you have to withdraw, such as when you feel your emotions getting the best of you. Other times it may be helpful to win, compromise or yield. If your pattern is mostly one of these, however, you're probably using it as a weapon.

WHAT DO YOU THINK?

1. Which weapon do you tend to use most?
   ___win ___withdraw ___compromise ___yield

2. Describe how you use this weapon in a typical conflict.

3. How does using this weapon affect the people you are in conflict with?

RESOLVING—THE CONSTRUCTIVE CREATIVE WAY

Our fifth choice when a conflict comes is not really a weapon. It is the art of resolving our conflict. Like any art, it takes time and practice (with a lot of errors) to learn. But if we learn how to resolve we can build conflict into a constructive, creative part of our relationships. Here's how:

1. **Listen more than you talk.** Instead of demanding that you be heard, listen carefully to your parents. Try to give them the feeling that you heard what they said and felt. (See Proverbs 18:13 and James 1:19). When parents feel that they have been heard, they are more likely to listen to what you are saying.

2. **Give conflict time.** Sometimes conflicts come up just before you or your parents are scheduled to leave. Trying to resolve them on the run or in a hurry just doesn't give anyone enough time to listen, think or be creative. In these situations it may be wise to leave the conflict hanging on for a while, making an appointment to talk it through when you have more time. Postponing like this is threatening if there's a fear of punishment involved or if there's a pattern of withdrawal. But try saying something like, ''Dad, could we talk about this somemore this evening when I get back? I'd like to tell you how I feel, too. But right now I've promised to pick up my sister at church. May I go?''

3. **Define the problem.** State as explicitly as you can what you think the problem is. Then see if you can state what you hear your parents saying the problem is. If you can define the problem as your

parents see it you have achieved a basic understanding that you can work from.

4. **Define your agreements and disagreements.** Sometimes these are not the same as the definition of the problem itself. Most of the time there are both areas of agreement and areas of disagreement. This will tend to make the problem a little more manageable.

5. Here comes the difficult part: **Identify your own contribution to the conflict**. A **few** conflicts may be one-sided, but most involve contributions from both sides. When you accept some responsibility for the conflict, your parents are likely to be much more open to discussion and cooperation.

You might say something like "Mom, I haven't been listening to you as carefully as I need to," or "Dad, I've let up on my part of the deal."

6. **Suggest what you can do to help solve the conflict.** Suggest more than one idea if possible. Give your parents a choice, and ask for their opinion. Then when a parent shares his or her opinion, be open to feelings, observations, and suggestions. Don't try to justify your position. Even if it seems at this point like you're copping out, you're not. You are offering to try new roads by suggesting creative alternatives.

7. **Suggest a way your parents could help you or a way you could help them.** This allows them to feel interdependent in the situation. It also, in a non-threatening way, allows them to choose to change something. Think, together, of as many possible solutions as you can. The more you think of, the more likely it is that you will find one that will be acceptable to all.

8. **Make a commitment to follow the solution or solutions you picked together**. Make this commitment even if your parents don't make one too. Your parents will see that you are earnest in your attempts to resolve conflict and are likely to trust you more in the future. If they get the feeling that your resolution was just a way to squirm out of a conflict they won't be ready to invest in resolution next time.

It takes work! It takes time. It takes energy. But constructive creative conflict is a great art and skill to possess. The first few times you try it you may have this book handy to remember the steps involved. That's O.K. Later it will become more natural and easy to remember.

WHAT IS YOUR PLAN?

1. **List the steps for resolving so that you have an outline to follow next time you have a conflict.**

1. _____

2. _____

3. _____

4. _____

5. _____

6. _____

7. _____

8. _____

2. (Respond to these questions after you've tried resolving a conflict once.)

   a. Which step was easiest?

   b. Did you stop short of step 8? If so, how could you get through this step next time?

   c. Which step was most difficult?

   d. How did your attempt at resolving affect your parents?

   e. How did you feel about yourself after the conflict was over?

3. Remember, good art takes practice. Resolution doesn't come easy. If you get discouraged, look up, then memorize Romans 15:1-7.

---

1. James G.T. Fairfield, **When You Don't Agree: A Guide to Resolving Marriage and Family Conflict** (Scottdale, Pa: Herald Press, 1977).

CHAPTER IX

On The Witness Stand

"Hi, Mom, what's for dinner?" said Diane as she set her school books down on the kitchen counter.

"I found a new meatloaf recipe. It will be ready in twenty minutes," answered her mom.

"Twenty minutes? Couldn't I eat any sooner? If I don't I'll be late to Bible study."

"Last week I had it done earlier and you didn't come home on time. We all ate cold food because we tried to accommodate your schedule. Since you've gotten involved at your church we haven't been able to plan on anything," her mom said angrily.

"O.K. I'll eat out on Wednesday nights. Then you don't have to worry about when to have dinner ready. I can go straight to church from school and just pick up a hamburger on the way."

"You know what your father and I think about you eating junk foods, but I guess that's better than some of the other things you could be into," was her mother's reply.

"O.K. I'll see you about 9:00," said Diane as she walked out the door enjoying her new freedom. "If Mom or Dad would only come to church with me they would understand why Bible study is so important," Diane thought. "But they're not Christians, so of course they won't understand the things of the Spirit."

WHAT DO YOU THINK?

1. **How effectively do you think Diane and her mom communicated with each other? What would you have said in this situation that Diane didn't say?**

2. **Based on what they said, what do you think is important to Diane, and what is important to her mom?**

A conversation that same evening began the same way between Bill and his mom.

"Hi, Mom, what's for dinner?" said Bill as he passed through the kitchen on his way to his bedroom where he put his school books on his desk.

"I found a new meatloaf recipe. It will be ready in twenty minutes," answered his mom when he got back to the kitchen.

"Twenty minutes? If I set the table would it help us eat any sooner?"

"Are you that starved?" asked his mom.

"No, there's a Bible study at church tonight and I'd like to be there on time—but I can be late if I have to."

"Last week I had it done earlier and you didn't come home in time to eat with us," his mom replied.

"I guess I've messed up your schedule several times lately, haven't I? I'm sorry to have caused you trouble—I don't mean to. Maybe I'm trying to do too much."

"No, we know you're busy and we appreciate your attitude about it. We just like to eat together as a family. Here's your salad. Why don't you start on that," Bill's mom suggested.

"If Mom or Dad would come to church with me they might see why I enjoy it so much," Bill thought as he ate. "But they don't enjoy everything I enjoy, maybe they would be turned off by it. I'm glad we're studying how to tell people about Jesus. Maybe when we're finished I can tell them why Jesus is important to me and what he has to offer them."

Bill was a little late for Bible study that night but his mom was happy to let him go because he had stayed to eat her meatloaf and talk with her for a few minutes.

WHAT DO YOU THINK?

1. **How effectively do you think Bill and his mom communicated with each other? What would you have said in this situation that Bill didn't say?**

2. **Based on what they said, what do you think is important to Bill, and what is important to his mom?**

3. **If these conversations are typical of Bill's and Diane's communication with their parents, which one do you think would be more likely to receive a positive response when discussing the claims of Christ with their parents? Why?**

CONGRUENT MESSAGES

It is natural for a Christian teenager to want his or her parents to also be Jesus' people. He has eternal life; he wants his parents to have it too. He is enjoying his church, Bible study, and worship; he wants his folks to enjoy these things too.

But sometimes this same teenager is the very one who is turning his parents off to Christ. This often happens because the teenager's messages to his parents are not congruent. One message he tries to get across is that Jesus, church, Bible study, etc. are good for a teenager. They help him become a better person. If he can persuade his parents that church is good for him, they will encourage his attendance and they may become interested themselves.

A second message teenagers unconsciously give is that because they have a relationship with God and their parents don't, Dad and Mom don't understand them anymore. This message is communicated indirectly, but usually quite forcefully, by maintaining an attitude of superiority and righteousness.

Sometimes, in an effort to be more ''Christ-like,''

a teenager cuts off communication with his family by refusing to participate any more in customs they enjoy but he considers wrong. We are not suggesting that a teenager should be involved in sin with his parents, just to keep communication open. But sometimes when a teenager takes a position that something his parents do is wrong, he is conforming to a Christian culture rather than to what the Bible says. For instance, Tom's family drinks beer with their hamburgers at their Saturday night family barbecues. Tom has always enjoyed this tradition, but suddenly, because of a message at church, he quits enjoying beer, the family barbecue, and by his attitude condemns the rest of the family.

WHAT DO YOU THINK?

1. What does the Bible teach about beer drinking?

2. What does your church teach about beer drinking?

3. Would you continue a Saturday night beer tradition (not getting drunk) to keep communication and friendship with your parents assuming they are not "born again"? Why or why not?

A third message teenagers get across is that if their parents went to church with them all family problems would be solved. This common message needs careful thought because if the teenager is really growing in Christ, he should be easier to live with, not harder. It is super-important for Christian teenagers with "unsaved" parents to notice and understand their own contributions to family conflicts. It is also very important to volunteer accountability, initiate communication, complete those chores and jobs that parents assign including school work, and build relationships between parents and friends including dates.

The important principle is that parents are more likely to be influenced to respond positively to Jesus if they see Him changing the way you live at home. They are less likely to respond to the Gospel if your message is not congruent with the way you live at home.

CONVERSATION ABOUT SALVATION

If your life and your message are congruent and your parents can see that you love them and you're growing, the day will come when they will be open to talk to you about Jesus. You know that day has come when they individually or together ask you about Jesus in a no-conflict situation. That means they are not trying to pick a fight over religion, check up on your activities, or compare religious beliefs. They have seen a change in you and you've become a representative of God to them. Are there some do's and don'ts for this situation? We believe so. Let's start with the don'ts.

DON'TS

1. **Don't drag them to church.** Church is for Christians. It is for worship, training, fellowship, proclamation, and redemption, and your parents won't understand those ministries yet. They will be uncomfortable in your church until they respond to Jesus. If your church is having some special evangelistic services let another adult invite your folks. If you

invite them they may feel over-pressured to respond and be turned off. Personal evangelism is usually better even though it may take longer.

2. **Don't expect your pastor to lead your parents to Christ.** Pastors are expected to be religious, so your folks are more likely to be defensive with him than with another businessman in your church. Besides, you probably already know the answers to the important questions your parents might ask. The questions you can't answer are not usually the ones that keep a parent from responding to Christ.

3. **Don't try to convince your parents of their need for Christ.** Let the Holy Spirit convince them. If you try to do this you will probably come off as judgmental and superior. Let them tell you they need Jesus and then simply tell them how to meet Him.

4. **Don't preach or quarrel over religious issues.** Avoid being the arbitrator on the morality of their ideas. Your parents might try to make you "the authority in religious and ethical matters in the home." If you accept this status they don't have to think about them and come up with their own decisions. When you discuss God, the Bible, the church or your beliefs, keep your answers short and ask them a lot of questions in response.

5. **Don't try to force a decision.** Questions such as "Where would you be if Jesus came back tonight?" are better asked by somebody outside your family. Let the Holy Spirit draw your parents to Jesus. You just be ready for the introduction.

6. **Don't leave tracts and pamphlets lying conspicuously around the house.** They will more likely be resented as clutter than read as information. Let your parents come to you for answers.

DO'S

1. **Trust God's Holy Spirit.** The Holy Spirit draws people to Jesus. The Holy Spirit convicts people of their sinfulness. Your ministry is to show your parents the benefits of a personal relationship with Christ. You do this by the way you live. This includes your communication with your parents. They don't expect you to be perfect, so don't expect yourself to be perfect. Just trust the Holy Spirit to display Jesus to your parents in your life.

2. **Verbalize your love and acceptance.** When you were younger, your parents assumed you loved them. But since you've become more independent they may question your love. Periodically they need to hear that you love them and think they are O.K. They will be able to understand God's love better if it comes through you.

3. **Know how to introduce somebody to Jesus.** At your church, find out ways you can use to show someone how to establish a relationship with Jesus. Don't be afraid to tailor someone else's outline to your parent's needs. Just be sure you know what the Bible says about salvation so you can quote it freely or find the appropriate passages quickly. And don't be afraid to admit that you don't know an answer to any of your parent's questions. Just let them know you'll find out and make a commitment to share your findings with them.

4. **Surround your parents with Christian love.** This means, first, that you love your parents. Secondly, bring your friends who love Jesus, and who you think will love your parents, home to be around you and your parents. Then see if you can get your folks

together with adults from your church who have similar interests as your parents. Let these adults know that your parents need Jesus, but that you're **not** expecting them to lead your folks to Christ—just demonstrate God's love.

5. **Pray for your parents.** You probably are already praying. You may continue for quite a while before they are ready to respond. They may never respond positively to Jesus. But don't give up. Remember it is the Holy Spirit's job to bring people to Christ.

WHAT IS YOUR PLAN?

1. **Are your messages congruent? Or do you need to change some areas of your life to back up what you want to tell your parents about Jesus? If so, what do you want to change?**

2. **Review chapters in this book that deal with communication. What suggestions do they give you about communication concerning your relationship with Christ? List 3-5 suggestions you can use.**

3. **Do you know how to introduce someone to Christ? Write an outline here for your conversation.**

CHAPTER X

Dressing, Driving, Dialing, Dating

How do you respond to the four words in the title of this chapter? Are any or all of them issues in your home? Dress and appearance, the use of the phone, radio, stereo, television, car and dating don't appear as isolated problems too often. Usually there are problems such as ability to trust, the growth of responsibility, communication gaps and personal problems that surface around the issues of dressing, dialing, driving, and dating. These deeper issues must be resolved before there will be a resolution of the surface issues. But the surface issues are so common that they deserve some thought.

Let's look at each issue in this chapter because some are problems teenagers are wrestling with. But involved in each issue are some principles that will help you grow, even though you may have settled that issue long ago.

CONFRONTING THE ISSUES

There are two traps to avoid when confronting issues such as dressing, dialing, driving and dating. One is that of manipulating and the other is that of complicating the issues. You can complicate these issues by making a big deal or a scene whenever you feel your liberties may be limited. Or you can complicate these issues by seeing your parents as old-fashioned and out of date. They may not wear the same styles you wear, listen to the same music, or agree with your dating practices, but they are living in the present and doing their best to cope with it. Treating them as antiques only makes them defensive.

Another common way of complicating the issues is to use them as springboards for quarrelling. Issues rarely get resolved when they turn into quarrels — they just get sidelined.

You manipulate your parents when you restrict their ability to choose. You can do this by employing any of the games mentioned in chapter four.

Each time any of these or other common issues arise, if you can keep two principles in mind you will probably be happier with the results.

Your parents want what they think is best for you. Before you quit reading and get sick, remember that even if your parents don't show you much love, you are, in their minds, an extension of their personalities. When you succeed in their eyes, they succeed. By the same token when they think you are behaving in such a way as to hinder your success **as they define it** they will usually hassle you. It is very difficult for parents to be objective in relationship to you for this reason.

Respond instead of reacting. Whenever one of the issues in this chapter arises, try to respond instead of reacting. The major difference between the two is that the responder thinks first, then says what he thinks while the reactor says what he feels like saying without thinking. The reactor acts like other people are responsible for what he says—**they** "make him" mad, happy, upset, jealous, etc. The responder knows that he is responsible for his emotions as well as his words and that only he can make himself angry, depressed, uptight, etc.

For instance, you walk into the living room just about ready to be picked up for a date wearing a new see-through blouse you bought for this date. Your dad takes one look at you and says, "No way—you can't leave this house lookin' like that!"

WHAT DO YOU THINK?

1. If you "reacted" to your dad's reaction what would you say?

2. If instead of reacting to your dad you "responded", what would you say?

Since there are somewhat different problems involved in each of the issues in our chapter title, let's discuss each of them, one at a time.

DRESSING

The clothes you choose to wear, the way you style your hair, the way you take care of your body—are all clues to what you think about yourself. In a sense, the way you appear is the way you advertise yourself to the world. If you want the people most important to you to think of you as a sexy person, you pick sexy clothes. If you think of yourself as an athlete, you pick athletic clothes.

Some men advertise themselves as businessmen by the suit and tie they choose. Women's apparel and makeup are deliberately designed to "accent" or "hide", to "round and shape" or to "lift and separate" and advertise certain features a woman considers important. Teenagers' clothes are made and chosen to advertise, too. T-shirts and sweatshirts even use pictures and words to advertise the ideas, philosophy, or wants of their wearers.

How are you advertising yourself? If your parents don't like the way you dress, maybe it's because they are afraid of the image you are building for yourself. We are **not** suggesting that your parents should choose your clothes for you. We do suggest that when you choose clothes, hair styles, etc. that you ask yourself, and maybe even your mom or dad what that particular piece of clothing says about you.

In asking the "advertising question" you might consider one more thing, too—false advertising. False advertising on T.V. can lead to lawsuits. But many people falsely advertise themselves all the time by clothes they choose. Guys and gals will buy and wear clothes deliberately designed to say "I'm available for sex" when they have no intention of having sex at all.

Consider sitting down with your folks and clearing the air. Talk about how you want to advertise yourself and why, and get their response. Talk about the messages your parents are receiving. You might even talk about the messages you are receiving from your parents by the clothes they choose. Then you might go shopping for new clothes—together!

WHAT DO YOU THINK?

1. **What are you advertising by the clothes and appearance you choose?**

2. **What other aspects of your personality could be accented by a change in style of dress or appearance?**

3. **If you were to choose and buy each of your parents an outfit, what would your purchases tell you about your wishes for them?**

DIALING

Whether it's over the T.V., the telephone, the stereo, the radio or another instrument, you've probably had some family hassles involving dialing. Most families do sooner or later.

Some families avoid hassles over dialing by simply buying their teenagers their own phones, stereos, T.V.s, etc. But before you say, "great idea!" think about some questions. Wouldn't having your own phone, T.V., stereo, etc. allow you to ignore your family most of the time? Wouldn't these electronic devices become escape mechanisms? Wouldn't it be better in the long run to deal with your problems and family problems together?

The key to resolving dialing problems is communication and consideration. Do your folks complain that you're on the phone too much or too long? Maybe they've wanted to use the phone several times while you've been on an extended call to one of your friends. You've probably been unable to use the phone sometimes when one of your parents was on an extended call. Why don't you take the initiative and get a five minute timer. Limit your calls to five minutes and decide that anything that's going to take longer can better be handled in person. This won't always work but it will work most of the time, and your consideration for your folks will be rewarded sooner or later.

How about the stereo, T.V. or radio? Do your folks object to your taste in programs, music and records? Here again communication and consideration will help resolve the hassle. Try asking them why they like the music and programs they like. Show a real interest—you might learn some things about your folks! Don't criticize their taste or you'll open yourself up to their criticism of yours. Instead, you might consider their taste and put their music or programs on when you're together.

Sometimes it's not a matter of taste but of morality. A lot of music and T.V. programming needs to be X-rated. But rating music and programming is much better done **with** each other rather than **for** each other.

Maybe a ''dialing covenant'' could be worked out

with your parents. If you've been hassled a lot over dialing, why not suggest it. A dialing covenant is an agreement your family works out and signs so that everybody is aware of the rules you've set up together. It might include a weekly planning time or family council, a sign-up sheet, a telephone log, the changes in schedules that friends in your home might make, limits on total weekly time on the T.V., stereo or phone or a quality review system like Philippians 4:8. The important thing is that you work out the convenant together.

DRIVING

Driving becomes an issue for almost every family some time prior to the age each state sets for minimum eligibility. The ability to drive sets you free in so many ways that it's something just about every teenager looks forward to.

Aquisition of a driver's license can be a time of growth, especially in responsibility, or it can be a time of regression to playing with new toys—only the toys can now kill. If you are looking forward to driving, you might suggest a "driving covenant" to your parents. This way most of the hassle that so often involves use of the car can be worked out ahead of time in calm communication rather than in last minute concessions.

A couple of years ago one of our family's best friends put together a driving covenant. Sheryl was going to get a driver's license, so she and her parents took several months of communication to put together their covenant. It saved an awful lot of hassle and made learning to drive an adventure for the whole family.

DATING

Of all the issues in this chapter, dating is the one most likely to be at the center of most hassles. The questions that surround the areas of dating and sexual standards are often areas of non-communication in Christian homes. One survey found that 91% of 200 college students said parents had given them no instruction about dating; and 43% no instruction whatsoever on sex (Homemade, May 1977).

Parents often assume that their teenagers are getting correct answers to their questions outside their home. You may be getting correct answers, but you may also be getting half-truths, misinformation, and ideas that will have very negative consequences for your future, especially if it includes marriage. Some parents assume that their teenagers don't need information on dating and sex until they discover it themselves. Others are simply afraid to talk about dating and sex because they have hang-ups of their own in these areas or they don't want hassles with you.

You need all the accurate information you can get on dating and sex. Since whole books have been written on these topics we won't try to deal with them here. But may we suggest the following excellent resources: **Before You Say, "I Do"** by Norman Wright, (Harvest House Publishers, 1978), **Sex and the Bible**, a cassette 2-pack by Norman Wright (Denver, Co.: Christian Marriage Enrichment, 1975), **A Love Story** by Tim Stafford (Zondervan, 1977). There are many other helpful resources in Christian bookstores.

Let me suggest a great way of getting the information you need and building your communication and relationship with your parents at the same time.

First write yourself a short list of questions you want answers to. Don't overwhelm anybody with a long list. You can repeat this procedure.

Second, on an evening when you have some time with both of them, ask your parents the first question. Preface your questions with something like this: "Dad, Mom, I have several questions I'd like to ask you. I need your information and opinions. Can you give them to me now or should I ask again later?" With a preface like this you let your parents know you want to talk, you have several questions not just one, what you want from them, and you give them a choice. If they choose to postpone the discussion ask them when would be a good time for it.

Third, at your nearest Christian bookstore, buy one of the resources listed on the previous page. You might start with Staffords, **A Love Story.** Read it and as you do so, write down questions you would like to ask your folks. Ask them to read it and write down questions they would like to ask you.

Fourth, set aside a regular time to discuss your reading.

Fifth, consider putting together a dating covenant. Discuss your dating ideas, beliefs, values, attitudes and practices with your parents. They may help you, they may not. But I'll bet that if you're willing to communicate about dating, your parents will understand you better and hassle you less.

WHAT DO YOU THINK?

1. **What do you and your parents understand the objectives of dating to be?**

2. What are your expectations of dating behavior? For example, is the guy expected to see how far he can go sexually? Is the girl supposed to be the one to decide on limits? Who is expected to decide what time to be home?

3. Are your expectations any different because of your relationship with Christ from what they would be without Him?

4. What qualities do you have to offer a person you might date?

5. How does a girl pick her dates? Should she be passive and wait for a guy to ask her out? Why?

6. What qualities do you look for in the persons you date?

WHAT IS YOUR PLAN?
1. Which of the issues discussed would be worth your

time and thought to work on? Are there similar issues like the use of money or your own apartment or schooling that need to be thought through?

2. If you and your parents were to work out a covenant in the area that is now an issue, what would be important items to include? Be sure you respond to this question instead of reacting.

3. What items do you predict your parents would insist on in this covenant, and how do you respond to these items?

4. Try it—start a conversation with your folks about a covenant—and if they respond positively, give yourselves time to work out the details. A covenant is too important to complete quickly.

CHAPTER XI

Friends

Close your eyes and think about your friends for a minute. See if you can picture their faces on the inside of your eyelids.

Maybe you saw the face of the guy or girl who lives on your block and has been your friend since the fourth grade. He's been in your house almost as much as in his own. Maybe you saw your church group, or the guys on the basketball team.

How do your parents see your friends? Which of your friends do they seem to prefer? Which of your friends seem to threaten your folks or cause them anxiety?

THE BIBLE ON FRIENDS

The Bible has much to say about friendships. The nature of God's relationship to His people and how we can enjoy that relationship is central to the whole Biblecal message. There are many examples of beautiful friendships in Scripture. David and Jonathan, Paul and Silas, Paul and Philemon, Moses and Jethro, Barnabas and John Mark are all friends you've probably heard about in Sunday School. Studying friendship in Scripture is something your family might enjoy doing together and it would be a great learning experience.

The book of Proverbs speaks to the issue of friendship in two ways.

First, Proverbs is a book about wisdom and character. It distinguishes between the wise and the foolish, between the person with character and one who will bring ruin on himself and others. The Proverbs, then can be a yardstick for measuring and choosing friendships.

Secondly, the book of Proverbs deals with friendship and the choice of friends specifically. Some aspects of friendship it deals with are:

1. Determing what kind of friends your friends are—Proverbs 9:7-9, 10:8-11, 17:4-5, 17:17, 19:22, 20:11.

2. Choosing friends carefully—Proverbs 13:20, 20:6-7, 27:17, 28:7, 29:24.

3. Avoiding some "friends"—Proverbs 14:7, 18:24, 20:19, 22:24-25, 23:20-21, 29:3.

WHAT DO YOU THINK?

1. **Would you include your parents in your list of friends?**

2. **How do you continue to build your friendship with your parents? Or do you take their friendship for granted?**

YOU AND YOUR FRIENDS

The friends you choose will not only have an impact on you but on your whole family as well. This may be obvious if your friends hang out at your house. But it is also true even if your family sees very little of your friends.

Often parents blame their teenagers' friends for separating their family and hurting their relationships. "They are such a bad influence on my Jimmy," is a mother's complaint. She may have a valid complaint, but maybe it can be remedied.

JIM, HIS DAD AND LARRY

Jim and his dad have had a fairly stable and strong relationship over the years. Jim has changed a lot as he grew, and so has his relationship with his dad. But it has remained positive.

In high school Jim makes a lot of new friends, one of which is Larry. At first, Jim's dad accepts Larry as he has most of Jim's friends. But soon he begins to feel that Larry is a bad influence on his son, so he begins looking for ways to keep them apart. Jim and Larry resent this, of course, so the pressure for someone to change builds.

Jim's dad feels the pressure of a dilemma. If he says nothing and lets Larry keep influencing Jim, he figures that Jim will absorb many of Larry's attitudes and values and will alienate himself from his family. On the other hand, if he fights Jim's friendship with Larry, he may fuel Jim's resentment and alienation.

Jim feels pressure from Larry to invest less in his home and parents and more in activities geared to his own age. Jim also feels pressure from his dad to invest less in Larry and more in his home and family.

Larry even feels some pressure from Jim's dad to change or be cut off from Jim's family.

WHAT DO YOU THINK?

1. **If you were Jim would you:**
   a. **Confront your dad about his attitude toward Larry?**
   b. **Get angry with your dad for trying to interfere with your choice of friends?**
   c. **Drop your friendship with Larry if your dad asked you to?**
   d. **None of the above; I would** _____

   _____

2. **How would your dad and mom respond to the solution you picked?**

It might be helpful at this point to consider the nature of friendships. Blaming Larry for changes in Jim's attitudes and values won't help Jim, his dad or Larry. The idea that a teenager rebels because of the influence of his friends is as old as Pinocchio, but it is not realistic. Friends may help a person express rebellion and may introduce new ways to rebel, but we all choose friends to complement the attitudes and values we already have.

One author on friendship states this principle this way: "You are your friends in many ways. They reflect your moods and your characteristics, your weaknesses and strengths, and they very realistically indicate your needs, some of which you yourself may not be aware of. Looking at your friends individually and collectively, a pattern emerges, and that pattern can be a highly accurate barometer of your emotional state." [1]

In the situation of Jim, his dad and Larry, Larry would be a fairly accurate indicator for both Jim and his dad of what's going on in Jim's life.

A second consideration about friendships is that we all want the people we choose as friends to be friends to each other as well. There is a natural tendency to be inclusive with friends of friends. "Any friend of yours is a friend of mine" expresses this. A parents' friends are automatically expected to be their teenagers' friends as well, even though this is often unrealistic.

Taking Jim, his dad and Larry again, let's diagram their relationship.

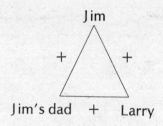

Since Jim and his dad are friends, when Jim develops a friendship with Larry the natural tendency is for Jim's dad and Larry to be friendly toward each other.

But if Larry reflects some of Jim's attitudes and values that Jim's dad doesn't like, not only does he change his attitude toward Larry but the whole "triad relationship" changes.

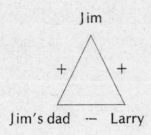

Notice the algebraic product of the signs in the diagram. If you remember from your algebra class (assuming you've taken algebra), two pluses times a minus equals a minus. Whether you followed that or just figured it out from the description, the important thing is that this triad relationship is out of balance. There is pressure on all three persons in the triad relationship to change in some way to balance the relationship.

WHAT DO YOU THINK?

1. If you are in an unbalanced triad relationship with your parents and one of your friends, try asking your parents just what it is they don't like about your friend. Their answer will let you know some areas in your life you will need to work on. Don't defend your friend or yourself, just listen carefully. Are you gutsy enough to try this?

To go back to our illustration, Jim's dad and Larry might find a way of accommodating each other, thereby changing their negative relationship into a positive one and balancing the triad relationship again.

Another way of balancing the triad relationship again is if the relationship between Jim and his dad becomes negative.

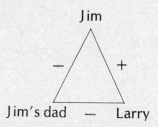

A plus times two minuses equals a plus or balanced relationship. Unfortunately this is the experience many families share. As teenagers acquire their own friends their relationship with their parents becomes negative. In fact many teenagers expect this alienation and see it as a natural part of growing up. But even though the development of independence is a natural part of growing up and acquiring your own friends is a part of this process, parent-teen alienation is not necessary.

The third way of balancing the triad is to keep your relationship with your parents positive even at the expense of some of your relationships with your friends. It would look like this:

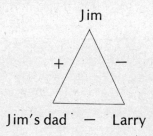

HANDLING FRIENDSHIP PRESSURES

Whenever triad relationships are out of balance there is pressure on one or more people in the relationship to change. Since it's your friends and your parents who are involved, there will be more pressure on you to change than on either your parents or your friends. How do you handle this pressure?

One way to handle friendship pressure is to live with it. Realize it will probably get worse than it is now, and that you stand the risk of losing one or more friendships anyway. But if you can handle the pressure of being a friend to two people who can't stand each other, eventually one of the two people will feel enough pressure to change. Either your dad might change and accept your friend or your friend might change and accept your dad.

Independence means that you are not seeking to get some of your needs met through your friendship. For instance, people who feel worthless tend to build friendships with people who make them feel worthwhile. They become dependent on these friends to feel worthwhile. One reason families exist is to mutually meet each other's needs. Some teenagers fight for independence from their parents for years only to become dependent on friends who love them far less than their parents do.

If you choose as friends people whose needs you can meet, then take the initiative to meet those needs. In the process, you will gain independence, build many meaningful relationships and loyalties and leave the pressure to change on other people.

A realization of who you are is important in finding friends who will help you rather than manipulate you. When you are trying to find out who you are you leave yourself open to pressure from people to become what **they** want you to be rather than being yourself.

Leadership means that you set the pace enabling others to follow rather than going along with the crowd. Not everybody is going to follow you but taking initiative to go where **you** want to go at least gives other teenagers an alternative. You don't have to "fit in." Give others a chance to fit in with you!

A second way to handle friendship pressure is to have lots of friends who are different from each other. It may feel more secure to belong to a gang that holds the same values, attitudes, beliefs, appearance and behavior. But be a friend to more than one kind of person. Don't let "the gang" choose your friends for you—choose your own friends.

Third, build a strong relationship with your parents. If they feel your love and respect they will be far less likely to hassle you over your friend-ships than if they feel you don't love or respect them. Invest in your parents. Continually develop com-munication. Actively love, trust and accept them even when you disagree with them.

Fourth, communicate your values as clearly as possible to both your friends and your parents. Try to sell your values to your friends and even your par-ents. Rather than overwhelming people with the logic of your values and the shortsightedness of theirs, make your values an attractive investment. Communication is the key to your parents—and your friends!

WHAT IS YOUR PLAN?

1. What are some things you can do to build or re-build your relationship with your parents?

2. Pick one of the things you listed in number one and answer the following questions. These will help you make it work.
    a. What aspect of your relationship with your dad or mom do you want this action to build?

    b. What will you try to communicate to your parents?

    c. When is a good time to try it?

3. Would your parents be open to the idea of investing together with you in one of your friends? How can you suggest this idea?

---

1. Jerry Gilles, **Friends—The Power and Potential of the Company You Keep** (New York: Coward, McCann & Geoghegan, 1976, p. 15)

CHAPTER XII

Responsibility

What's your response to responsibility? Chances are you have have mixed feelings about it—most teenagers and even young adults do. Some people eagerly accept responsibility; even hunt it down. Others avoid it like acne. Some responsibilities are easier to welcome; like staying out later at night, weekend trips with friends, use of the family car or your own car. Other responsibilities taste more like milk of magnesia; like paying some of the monthly bills, helping little brother through school, or upkeep of the house and yard.

What is responsibility? Is it an innate quality inherited from parents? Is it born of adversity? Is it the same thing as self-discipline? Responsibility is defined differently by different people. Maybe a working definition would be that **responsibility is an ability to respond maturely**. It is not quite the same as maturity because very young children can sometimes be responsible. But as people are given responsibility they tend to mature. Responsibility is not quite the same as self-discipline because very self-disciplined people can act irresponsibly sometimes and impulsive people can often be very responsible.

How do people, especially teenagers, become responsible?

Three things that concern most teenagers and their parents makes a difference in the rate of growth of responsibility. These three things are 1) your development from dependence to independence; 2) your development in discipline from parental-discipline to self-discipline; 3) the relationship between growth in independence and self-discipline and your parents' expectations.

If you're a junior higher, even though you might wish otherwise, you are still quite dependent on your parents for money to buy clothes, records and anything else. You must also depend on them for transportation to any place out of bicycle or skateboard range. If you're in college you are probably earning the money you need for clothes, dates, car, etc. You probably make your own decisions about when to come home at night, you've made some major choices concerning school and a major and you're faced with many more immediate and important decisions.

WHAT DO YOU THINK:

1. How far have you come in growth toward independence? The point at the left end of the line at the top of page 137 represents the dependence you had as a seventh grader and the point at the right end represents the independence you will

**have when you are 20. Put an X on the line at the
point of growth where you think you are
presently.**

_____

DEPENDENCE   INDEPENDENCE

2. **Next, put a D on the line at the point you guess
   your dad would put you, and an M at the point you
   guess your mom would put you.**
3. **On a separate piece of paper, draw the same line
   with the two end points, the words ''dependence''
   and ''independence'' but without your X, D, or
   M. Then describe to each of your parents what
   the line means reading number one above if you
   need to. Ask them to put a D and an M where they
   think you are. Then compare it with your guesses.**

_____

If your parents marked you differently from your
own mark, don't be surprised. The way they define
dependence and independence will probably be a
little different from the way you see it. Secondly,
they feel differently about your independence at different times depending pretty much on how self-
disciplined you are.

Most junior high young people do ''what needs to
be done'' things like chores, practices, fixing up the
house, taking care of clothes, etc. because their
parents will ''discipline'' them if they don't. By the
time young people are in college, their parents hope
they will be self-disciplined enough to ''do what they
have to do'' on their own. Clues to parents that their
teenager is growing in self-discipline are the care of
his room and clothes, discharge of his family duties
without reminders, keeping his word (especially

about return times on dates), and the kinds of choices he makes.

WHAT DO YOU THINK?

1. **As you did with dependence-independence, put an X on the line below to indicate your growth in self-discipline.**

  •————————————————————————•

PARENTAL DISCIPLINE   SELF-DISCIPLINE

2. **Put your parents' initials on the line where you think they would put you.**
3. **Compare their opinions with your guesses and your X.**

Your growth in independence and in self-discipline are a major part of your relationship with your parents, like it or not. Most parents will allow increasing amounts of independence if they feel that their teenagers are ready for it. So parents are primarily concerned about growth in self-discipline. On the other hand most teenagers are less concerned about growth in self-discipline than the independence they see their peers attaining and feel they themselves need.

How about you? In the graph on page 139 you have growth in independence on the horizontal line and growth in self-discipline on the vertical line. Put your X marks from the first two ''What do you think'' sections onto the horizontal and vertical lines. Straight up from your X on the horizontal line, and straight across from your X on the vertical line put a dot. Now draw a straight line from your dot to the bottom left corner where the vertical and horizontal lines meet. The line you just drew represents your growth in responsibility. Is this line closer to being horizontal or vertical?

Self-Discipline |

Parental Discipline |

Dependence   **Independence**

The next step is crucial. On a separate sheet of paper draw the diagram above without your X's and line. Take it to your parents, one at a time, and ask them to put an X on the horizontal line indicating how independent they think you are and an X on the vertical line indicating how self-disciplined they think you are.

Straight up from their X on the horizontal line and straight across from their X on the vertical line put a dot, and draw a line down to the left-hand corner. Let's call this line your ''parents expectation'' line.

Now compare your ''parents' expectation line'' with your ''growth in responsibility line'' you drew in this book. If your parents' line is more vertical than your responsibility line don't be surprised. It means that your parents expect you to do some growing in self-discipline **before** they will give you much more independence.

If you want your parents to give you more freedom and independence you will have to show them that you are self-disciplined enough to handle it. In other words, your line of responsibility needs to be more vertical than your parents' line of expectation for awhile. The result will soon curve down to a more horizontal direction as they begin to think of you as a more responsible person.

EARNING INDEPENDENCE

Some teenagers fight for freedom—hassling their parents long enough until they give in and let their teenagers do whatever they want. But you will be better off earning your freedom instead of fighting for it for several reasons.

1. When you earn your freedom you learn self-discipline and you become far more responsible as an individual. Responsibility will be one of your greatest assets for the rest of your life if you can grow in it now.

2. Freedom comes much quicker to those who earn it than to those who fight for it. Fighting for independence naturally makes your parents fight against giving you freedom. Sometimes they continue fighting you long after you've quit fighting— that's too bad.

3. Why fight for your freedom anyway, if there's an easier way of getting it? Fighting is a hassle, especially when you're fighting someone you love.

You can learn self-discipline and earn independence. **The basic ingredient is willingness to figure**

out what the people around you, especially your parents, need and how you can meet their needs. Figuring out parents' needs is the easy part—most parents tip you off in many ways. When they hassle you about something, for instance, they are coming from a need that hasn't yet been met. Some of these needs are obvious. For instance, if your dad hassles you over the volume on your stereo, his obvious need is for less volume. Behind that need may be some more needs like rest (maybe he's been working too hard), peace (maybe his boss has been hassling him) or a chance to express his feelings without being rushed or drowned out by the music.

Once you've figured out some of your parents' needs pick one that you can do something about, and without a word do what you can. Your folks may notice what you did and comment on it, or they might not. Don't get discouraged if they don't notice what you did. Do something else for them. Your goal is not to get them to notice your good deeds, it is to demonstrate over a period of time that you are growing in self-discipline. They will get the feeling that you are growing if you keep working at it consistently. Even though they don't notice all the things you do, hang in there.

Observe family rules and avoid the limits. Some families are careful to have family rules written down and posted. Other families don't communicate rules so clearly. If your family doesn't have written rules, you may be getting into hassles because you aren't sure what your parents really expect. Here's a suggestion: Sit down and write a list of family rules you think are operating in your home. Then pick a time when you can talk for a while with both your parents together. Read each rule and talk about it one at a time. Some rules may be for younger brothers and sisters, not you. Other rules may be ready to be dropped. Some you may have forgotten and will add to your list.

Once you are sure about your family rules, make them a priority, and avoid even coming close to breaking them. For instance if being at home by 11:00 on weeknights is one of your family rules, make sure you're home by 10:30!

Take the initiative to communicate. Don't expect your parents to always be the conversation starters, especially about serious things. Talk **with** them. Ask them questions. Show them you are open to their opinions and ideas even if some of these ideas are outmoded. Try to express your feelings, values, judgment, beliefs, etc. in their language. Review the chapters in this book on communication and listening if you need to make these conversation times a little smoother. But take time to communicate.

Try not to make promises you can't keep. Sometimes parents, as well as other people, want you to do something and are afraid you don't want to do it. So they ask you to promise you will do it. They even bug you until you promise. Then if you can't keep your promise, even though it's not your fault, they will send you on a guilt trip. At the same time they assume you can't be trusted because you are acting too young or immature.

If your parents are asking you to do something and you have an idea that you just might not be able to come through well ahead of time, here's an alternative. Instead of making that promise tell your folks that you really want to do what they are asking you to do and that you will try your best. But tell them you're afraid to promise that it will get done because something may prevent it and you would rather not promise than promise and fail.

Avoid appeals to fairness. "Jimmy got a present and I didn't," or "All the kids at school are doing it," are appeals to fairness. You can probably think of many others. By appealing to fairness you encourage your parents to think of you as a child rather than as a young adult. Realize that your parents can't be exactly fair all the time but that doesn't mean they don't love you. Give them the freedom to express their love to you in ways they have to duplicate for your brother or sister. When your parents are unfair don't make a big deal of it. Let it go and realize that sooner or later you'll probably be on the advantage end of something that's unfair to someone else.

Admit mistakes and apologize. Learning from your mistakes is much more mature than denying them. When you admit mistakes your parents don't have to prove you made them. The time and energy your parents spend proving you blew it only reinforces in their mind the idea that you make lots of mistakes because you're irresponsible.

WHAT IS YOUR PLAN?

1. **In what areas of home life have you been responsible? List them.**

2. What are some of your parents' needs you suspect you could meet? List them.

3. Which of these needs can you meet, and how will you go about meeting them?

4. Can you think of some other ways you can demonstrate self-discipline and earn independence? List them here.

_____